Midwestern Pioneers
Second Generation

My Mother's Stories of Growing up on a Kansas Farm, Early 1900's

Written by
Ruth Carlson Wareham

Edited by Ruth's daughter, Linda Metz Scales
Illustrations by Rhian Swain

Fulton Books
Meadville, PA

Published by Fulton Books 2022

ISBN 978-1-63985-827-9 (paperback)
ISBN 979-8-88505-967-1 (hardcover)
ISBN 978-1-63985-828-6 (digital)

Printed in the United States of America

Contents

Foreword v

Acknowledgments vii

Chapter 1:   Conestoga Wagon Trip to Kansas 1

Chapter 2:   Father, Victor Emil Carlson 5

Chapter 3:   Early Days on the Family Farm 10

Chapter 4:   Country School 15

Chapter 5:   Chores 19

Chapter 6:   The Older Kids and Cars 23

Chapter 7:   The Garden 25

Chapter 8:   Threshing Time 28

Chapter 9:   The Day the Gypsies Came 32

Chapter 10: Every Day Is a Busy Day 35

Chapter 11: Tasting Soap 40

Chapter 12: Peddlers…and Doctors 42

Chapter 13: Sunday—a Day of Rest? 44

Chapter 14: Grown Up 46

Foreword

Have you wondered what your parents were like as children? Where did they grow up, and what was the world like where they grew up? What were the national events that had an impact on them?

My mother, Ruth Lucille Carlson (Metz) Wareham, wrote stories of her growing up on a farm in North Central Kansas as part of a second generation of pioneers. She spent many years without indoor plumbing and no electricity, phones, radios, television, or cars. In 1985, she typed (yes, typed) many of her own stories so we would better understand her world.

I am very pleased for you to meet my family.

Linda Metz Scales

Acknowledgments

This book is a compilation of stories my mother wrote with very few editorial additions by me. I received the gift of life from my mother, and she also gave me a life of unconditional love. She was a courageous, resourceful, gracious, fun-loving woman, and I am so proud of her.

I wish to thank the very talented artist, Rhian Swain, for providing the wonderful illustrations. I also like to thank my loving husband, retired episcopal Army chaplain Lou Scales; my very special daughters—Gelene Frey-Tabor and Jennifer Frey; and my dear friend Jane Ellis for editing the stories and providing lots of encouragement. I'm blessed, and I'm grateful.

Chapter 1

Conestoga Wagon Trip to Kansas

What was it like to grow up on a farm in Republic County, Kansas, at the turn of the twentieth century? I'll introduce you to my parents, Victor Emil Carlson and Margaret Louise (Bell) Carlson, and their parents, who were the first of our family to settle in Kansas. They paint the picture of pioneer life on a farmstead. Mother's father, William J. Bell, came to the United States with his parents from Glasgow, Scotland, in 1844 when he was a baby. William grew to be tall, thin, and good-looking. He loved to dress well and drove a team of handsome horses. He became a US citizen in 1891.

Mother's grandmother, Louisa Fancher, made an amazing trip to get to Scandia, Kansas, from Fond du Lac, Wisconsin, in 1863. Mother's grandfather, Jay Fancher, had a strong desire to explore and decided he would like to try his fortune in the territory of Kansas. He wanted to check out the area before transplanting his family to Kansas. He and a neighbor, Mr. Sweat, decided to visit Scandia together because they shared an interest in exploring Kansas. Before they left, they told their wives, "We'll get a letter to you as soon as we can. If we find it's a nice place, we want you to join us there. We already have horses here. You get wagons and load them with food that won't spoil like potatoes, carrots, flour, sugar, and coffee. Bring what you can and join the next wagon train that goes out that way."

The women did as they were instructed when the letter came, and they made their preparations for the journey. Early on the morning they were to leave, Mrs. Sweat knocked at Great-Grandmother Fancher's door. "Louisa, I'm so sick…" she moaned. "I just can't climb into that covered wagon this morning. Let's try it tomorrow. We can hurry and catch the wagon train by the end of the day. You know they don't move very fast."

So the next morning, they started their long journey—a sickly Mrs. Sweat with her 15 year-old son and a 13-year-old daughter along with Grandmother Fancher, 17 year-old Charley, 15 year-old Della, and 13 year-old Hattie Marie. Hard as they tried, they could not catch up to the wagon train the next day, the second day, or the third day. Late one afternoon, after a week or so on the trail, they found a clearing that looked like a desirable spot to make camp for the night. The boys unhitched the teams and staked them out to graze. The women started a fire and were preparing the evening meal.

"Mama," called Charley, "John and I are going to look around. We're going to the top of that rise ahead and see what we can find. Maybe we'll get a rabbit."

A half hour later, the women were busy cooking when they heard the boys run toward them as fast as they could travel.

"Indians!" Charley gasped. "Indians! We saw…"

The women shuddered.

"We saw…" he wheezed, "a rack with fresh meat on it to dry. They'll be back, Mama. They'll be back. We gotta move!" (A rack was two forked sticks driven into the ground, set a short distance apart, with a sapling laid across the forks. The meat hung from it to dry.)

The women were well aware of the urgent need to move in a hurry. They tried to not make a sound as they put out the fire, reloaded all the supplies into the wagons, hitched the horses to the wagon, and started out. They kept going until it was completely dark before stopping to spend the night. There was no fire and no warm meal. They ate a few bites of cold food in a hurry and went to bed. No one slept well that night.

The next morning, they quickly left just at daylight. Whenever they saw a hill on the trail ahead, they sent Charley or John to the brink to report whether they could see Indians. They kept a fast pace until they were certain the Indians they had almost encountered were far behind.

After some time, they slowed to a normal traveling pace and eventually reached their destination—the little town of Scandia on the Republican River. They never did catch the wagon train that was to have been their guide and protection for the long journey overland. These strong pioneer women and their children made the long trip from Wisconsin to Kansas unescorted. Wagon trains could travel from ten to fifteen miles per day depending on weather and other circumstances. At this rate, it would have taken from three to four months to make the trip.

The young girl who made this covered-wagon-ride trip to Kansas, Hattie Marie Fancher, married William J. Bell, who had come to the States with his parents from Glasgow, Scotland. Their first child was Margaret Louise Bell, my mother.

How did the Bell family get established on a farm? They benefited from the Homestead Act, which was one way settlers acquired land in Kansas. President Abraham Lincoln signed this law on

May 20, 1862. Settlers could claim 160 acres of public land by paying a small filing fee, which gave them options:

1. Live on the property for five continuous years, build a residence, and grow crops.
2. Purchase land from the government at $1.25 an acre after living on the land for six months, building a home, and having started growing crops.
3. A soldier with two years of service could acquire the land after one year of residency.

Of course, the head of the household had to have the intention of becoming a citizen. This act led to eighty thousand acres of land being allotted by 1900.

The Bell family assumed a homestead from someone who did not complete the requirements. The Bells completed these requirements, and the Bell Farm was theirs.

Chapter 2

Father, Victor Emil Carlson

My father, Victor Emil Carlson, came to Scandia in 1883 with his parents, Karl Johan and Johanna Louise (Orbeck) from Mjolling, Sweden. The name on the immigration papers was the surname of Karlsjon. The overseas journey lasted thirty days. Father delighted in telling the story of an old Swede who arrived in New York, looked up at the skyscrapers, and exclaimed, "My, if this is New York, what must Lindsborg be like!" Lindsborg was a Swedish settlement in Northeastern Kansas and was known as Little Sweden, USA.

Some of the Carlson's neighbors in Sweden had also immigrated to the Scandia area. One of their best friends, the Aspegrens, lived a few miles south of Scandia. They arrived in the States about two years before the Carlsons. Victor liked to tell everyone, "You know, Leonard Aspegren and I were rocked in the same cradle in Sweden." Father stayed with the Aspegren family the first year they were in the States.

They came from Östergötland, the province next south of the one in which Stockholm is located. Carl Johan Carlson became a US citizen in 1884. There were rumors that Grandmother Carlson's parents had connections with Swedish royalty, but that was never verified.

Victor's parents had found life very difficult in Sweden. At that time, there was a terrible depression, and it was difficult to find food even for a small family. Their desire to come to the United States was so great that the physical effect was akin to homesickness, homesickness for a home they didn't yet have. The thirty-day crossing of the Atlantic was gladly undertaken for the sake of the opportunities on the other side.

Victor was eleven years old when he arrived in Scandia, Kansas, with his parents and younger sister, Hannah. This chubby, rosy-cheeked boy (as Dad described himself) could not speak English, so when school started, he was placed in the first grade. What a sight to see him in a room of six-year-olds! He soon learned the language and caught up with his age group. Victor was in the first class that graduated from Scandia High School in 1893.

Grandfather Carlson was a carpenter, and Dad worked alongside him while he was growing up. Grandfather and Dad built many of the large farmhouses that still grace the farmsteads on the river road south of Scandia. When Dad was in high school, he worked at Gulick's Dry Goods Store after school. He continued in that capacity for several years.

Mr. Gulick also owned a store in Nicodemus, Kansas, an all-Black settlement in Western Kansas. The community was established by African Americans after the Civil War and was made up of ex-slaves who fled the South in search of equality, freedom, and a chance to restart their lives. The opportunity to acquire land through the Homestead Act also had appeal.

One summer, Mr. Gulick sent Dad to work in the Nicodemus store. Dad had seen a Black person but had never conversed with one. He had to learn to adapt to a new environment. At his new job, he became friends with a young man who also worked for Mr. Gulick. Nicodemus was a very small settlement with few activities to interest the two youths. When they read that a county fair was to be held in a nearby town, they decided to hire a horse and buggy and find some entertainment. They arrived, found a place to tie the horse, then made a leisurely trip around the grounds. They stopped at stands to try their luck at throwing baseballs to win a prize. At one point late in the afternoon, they suddenly realized they were the only White people in the entire fair. Feeling awkward and out of place, they became frightened and hastened back home. There were no problems.

Victor and Maggie were married on September 12, 1896. Their heights—Maggie at 5'1" and Victor at 5'8"—and stoic pose in their wedding picture didn't give a hint of their courage and fortitude.

Victor had made arrangements to rent a house in Scandia. He and Maggie planned to travel by train to St Joseph, Missouri, for their honeymoon, where they would buy brand-new modern furniture for their new home. They intended to leave immediately after the ceremony for the depot where a train was scheduled to arrive. Something went wrong with the timing. Just as the minister reached the point of saying, "I now pronounce you," the train whistled. Luckily, the train crew had been alerted that a newlywed couple would be boarding, so they held the train while Victor and Maggie raced to the depot in their carriage. Their frantic boarding provided the highlight of the day to the passengers, and no one seemed to mind the delay.

Following their return, Victor and Maggie settled in their new home with the new modern furniture. Whenever there was a stage performance at the opera house or a special event at the high school auditorium, the Carlsons were requested to loan their classy modern furniture for the occasion.

My grandmother, Johanna, did not learn to speak English, and Mother Maggie (her daughter-in-law) did not speak Swedish. Yet each understood the other. When communications were not clear, actions helped clarify the situation. Once, when Grandma was visiting, Mother was ironing Dad's long-sleeved shirts. Grandma tried to tell Mother something that she couldn't understand. Grandma took one of Mother's freshly ironed shirts and rubbed the bosom and cuffs briskly between her hands to demonstrate that Mother should rub in more starch and rub it into the material. Of course, the rumpled shirt had to be redone, as did Mother's sunny disposition. She was still upset about it when she related the story many, many years later.

Mother's parents lived on the Bell Farm, and Mother and Dad often visited them, accompanied by their St. Bernard dog, who trotted along beside the buggy. When my brother, Archer, was born in 1896, Dad wrote a note to the Bells to tell them of the arrival of their new grandchild. He tied it to the dog's collar and sent him to the farm with the message. It wasn't as fast as a telephone, but given that there were no telephones accessible at that time, the dog served the purpose very well.

Mother and Dad had fond memories of this huge animal. Often, there were homeless tramps in Scandia who came to the back doors of many homes, asking for food. Sometimes Indians did the same. One day, the dog was chained to his doghouse in the backyard, dozing in the warm sunshine. It looked perfectly safe to the tramp who was searching for a handout. He knocked at the back door, which awakened the beast. Mother reached the door in time to see the poor tramp running at full speed, pursued by the monster dog dragging his doghouse across the yard.

As was common in rural areas, medical support was quite limited. This led to many early deaths. Grandmother Hattie Bell developed pneumonia and died at the young age of forty-nine in 1899. My folks' second child was named Hattie in her honor. Their third child was named after Uncle Charley, but he only lived a year, dying of whooping cough.

After Grandmother Bell died, Maggie and Victor moved in with Grandfather Bell. They lived at the Bell Farm about four years and then moved to the farm that I knew as home. This farm was located between two North Central Kansas towns: Courtland and Formosa.

Chapter 3

Early Days on the Family Farm

When the Carlson family moved to the farm, the house was a typical four-room frame building—too small to meet the needs of the growing family. The third child, Grace, arrived in July after the move in March 1904. Dad decided the house was really too small. Since he had worked with his father at carpenter work, he was able to enlarge the house to six rooms with a minimum of help. Two rooms were added, making three rooms along each side of a rectangle with a door leading to the next room in each case. What fun we had as children, racing 'round and 'round the whole house! The fun lasted until Mother tired of the racket and put a stop to it.

I, Ruth Lucille, arrived in this busy household on a wintry day in January 1912, the eighteenth of the month or thereabouts, the eighth of nine children. I was Mother's largest baby at ten pounds, but I was the smallest adult, only 5'1". My birth occurred at the farm home under the supervision of Dr. Snyder, who had been present for several other Carlson births.

As an adult, when I wrote to the Bureau of Vital Statistics for a copy of my birth certificate, it was discovered that Dr. Snyder had recorded my birth as having occurred on the seventeenth. Since Dad had recorded my birth in the family Bible under the date of the eighteenth, I assumed that was correct and always celebrated on January 18.

I can just see wiry little old Dr. Snyder sitting at his cluttered desk on a Sunday morning, trying to catch up on paperwork. He had to satisfy that new-fangled requirement that a record of all births be sent to Topeka. He scratched his head and tried to remember when he made the trip out to the

Carlsons', Tuesday or Wednesday? He wasn't sure. He wasn't even sure if he had made five, six, or seven trips to the Carlsons' to deliver babies.

When my youngest brother, John, was born, the family births spanned across many years. John was born in 1913, and my oldest brother, Archer, graduated from high school in 1914. Hattie, born in 1900, was four years younger than Archer, and Grace was four years behind Hattie, born in 1904. Two babies—Charley, born in 1902, and Irene, born in 1906—died in infancy of whooping cough and pneumonia. Addison was the older of the "second family" of our children—Addison (1908), Marguerite (1910), Ruth (1912), and John (1913).

My earliest recollections are of the sleeping arrangements when I was very young. Mother and Dad occupied the front bedroom. The two oldest brothers—Archer and Addison—shared a bedroom. Five of us slept in the third bedroom. My oldest sister, Hattie, "raised" me while Grace, my next-oldest sister, had primary care of Baby John. Grace, Baby John, and Marguerite slept in one bed in this room. Hattie and I slept in a folding bed that fascinated me. During the day, it was curtained off, so its use was not readily apparent. But at night, it unfolded to become a full-size bed, complete with bedding already in place.

Two rooms were used regularly—a small kitchen with a woodburning cookstove and the dining room, also with a woodburning stove. Each had a woodbox close to the stove. Two very small rooms opening into the kitchen were the pantry, where the cream separator was located, and the closet in which the icebox was placed. The living room was used only when we had company.

The only rooms that were heated in winter were the kitchen and the dining room. Unless we were expecting company, the living room was not heated. Dad and Mother were the first ones to get up in the morning, so there was always heat by the time we awakened. We'd scurry out to the stove, find the pile of clothes we'd left there the night before, and dress in the warmth of the dining room.

I still remember how hard it was to leave the warmth at night to go climb into an ice-cold bed. The double blankets helped only a little. Sister and I might have quarreled during the day, but she was a welcome friend at night, especially if her feet were warm.

At the end of the day, we always gathered in the dining room. This was Dad's time to relax. He prepared his evening by ensuring there were at least three apples in the fruit basket. If not, he'd go to the fruit cellar for a refill. Then he'd change into his sheepskin-lined slippers, sit in his rocking chair near the Coleman lamp on the dining table, and read.

He subscribed to the *Country Gentleman*, the *Youth's Companion*, and later, the *Farm Journal*. He read the *Kansas City Star* and *Kansas City Times* from the front page to the last page. These two daily newspapers were thoroughly digested each evening while munching three apples. For years, the *Star* ran installments of currently popular books, and Dad didn't miss one. Mother was usually mending, though sometimes she was reading. Dad was always the last one to bed.

When telephones were available, we had two telephones in the dining room. The Courtland Exchange installed one on the east wall. Courtland was located east of our home. The one on the south wall was the Formosa Exchange one. It cost ten cents to call Courtland on the Formosa telephone, hence the decision to save the long-distance fees. Whenever one of the neighbors had reason to contact someone with a Courtland telephone, they'd phone us with the request, "Will you call so-and-so and tell them I said such and such?"

On the Formosa phone, our ring was one long and two shorts. When the operator rang a number, all the phones on that line rang at the same time. You soon learned which ring belonged to which neighbor. You knew that three shorts was the Simmons' home, and you could listen to the conversation if you wished. This was not considered good etiquette, but it sure was fun. Often, there would be a line call. When something of interest to the whole neighborhood happened, the operator (central) would ring five longs and then announce the important event. It might be the time and place of someone's funeral or "The Ebright house is on fire. They need help!" It might be to notify people of a farm sale or the birth of a child.

With such a large family, Mother's first concern was preparing enough food for eight or nine people who consistently appeared at the table five times a day, expecting to be fed. Yes, the family followed the Swedish custom of having 10:00 a.m. and 4:00 p.m. coffee. "Coffee" always meant coffee plus an occasional sandwich and always cake, cookies, or pie. Dad contended "coffee" was a necessity in Sweden, where the workday often started at 4:00 a.m. and lasted until dark. Such a desirable tradition should not be broken.

When the men worked in the field, someone would take both forenoon and afternoon coffee to them. It was a great thrill when I reached the age of fourteen to be able to drive the Chevy a mile to the field with lunch for Dad and any others who might be helping him. I can still remember one of the first trips to the far side of the farm. I had to turn around in the middle of a dirt road. In attempting to back up, I went too far and backed into a barbed wire fence. That frightened me, but what concerned me most was the fact that the barbs were caught in the cover of the spare tire mounted on the rear and tore it. Apparently, Dad didn't discover it, and I didn't want to confess unless necessary.

Dad often had "hired men." They lived with us and ate all their meals with us, including lunches. One of the most memorable was Old Cy Walker. I have no idea if he had a home somewhere else, but he would appear and work for Dad several months at a time, especially during corn shucking season. Old Cy chewed tobacco, and there was always a brown streak from the corner of his mouth to his chin and brown spatters all over his shirt front. He would hide his tobacco in the back of the buggy. The older kids found it and tried it. They discovered the hot taste in their mouths was not to their liking.

We changed our long underwear once a week, usually on Saturdays when we took our baths. A sense of real freedom came with the first warm days of spring when we were able to shed that long underwear. Of course, we wore long cotton stockings year-round. How did we keep them up? We wore a garment called a panty waist. It was a vestlike affair of cotton worn over the long underwear.

Mother usually braided my hair. It was parted in the middle. A small braid started above each ear, then they were combined with the other sections of hair into one larger braid at the center back. For special occasions like a program at school, Mother would put my hair up in rags. The night before the big event, I sat on a low stool in front of her. She'd take a strip of cloth about an inch wide and eighteen to twenty-four inches long. I held one end of the cloth next to my scalp; Mother dampened my hair and wound it round and round the cloth. When she reached the end of the hair, the remaining cloth was then wrapped around the outside of the curl until it reached the scalp. There, the two ends were tied together. It wasn't comfortable to sleep on those rolls, but I was proud of my curls when I appeared on the platform next day.

We had a Sunday dress and usually two school dresses. The clothes we outgrew or the ones that were handed down too many times were the ones to which we changed when we came home from school. We changed immediately upon arrival and then started our chores in order to be finished by dark.

Chapter 4

Country School

School started for me after my fourth birthday, the fall of 1916. The schoolhouse was just across the corner from our farmstead, less than two city blocks. My sister Marguerite was two grades ahead of me at this point, and brother Addison a year ahead of her.

One of my early memories is of a snowy day while I was in the first grade. When we came home for dinner at noon, Mother wondered whether I should return because of the severe cold. Finally, she decided I might as well go. She wrapped a scarf completely around my head, covered my eyes with it, and assigned brother and sister to take me by the hand and lead me back to school. Their intentions lasted until we reached the edge of the yard. By that time, they were hurrying ahead. I walked off a bridge on the highway at the corner of the yard. I fell about ten feet to the ground below. Quite naturally, it knocked the breath out of me. Marguerite and Addison carried me back to the house, where I soon regained consciousness. Mother kept me home for the afternoon, and I recovered speedily. About the time brother and sister were due home from school at 4:00 p.m., Mother decided to play a trick on them and powdered my face with flour to make me look pale. We didn't fool anyone.

Apparently, my progress during the first year of school was satisfactory. The teacher decided I should be kept busy by completing the second grade during the first half of the following year and the third grade during the last half. Now the three Carlson kids were in three consecutive grades. No one dared flunk!

From September through April, our world revolved around two things: school and chores. School hours were 9:00 a.m. to 4:00 p.m. with the usual noon hour and recesses from 10:30 a.m. to 10:45 a.m. and 2:30 p.m. to 2:45 p.m. Chores started immediately after school just as soon as we could change out of our school clothes. The length of time it took to complete the chores depended on the diligence with which we pursued the task at hand.

Our country school, a one-room building, had three windows on each side and was heated by a coal-burning stove. A cistern supplied water. It had the usual outhouse "plumbing." The teacher was the janitor.

We ate dinner—the noon meal—at home and envied those who brought their lunches in shiny gallon syrup buckets. They had more time to play during the noon hour than we did.

Ours was a small school, usually seven to ten pupils. Ages varied, so many classes had only one member. Classes on a specific subject lasted about fifteen minutes. When the teacher announced, "Third-grade reading," the pupils involved gave their attention. Next was the command, "Turn," and we did. Then "Stand" and "Pass," at which time we marched to the recitation bench. This was a long seat near the teacher's desk where the class was conducted. The pupils learned to concentrate because all classes were conducted in the same room.

Sometimes on Friday afternoon, we would have a spelling match, a ciphering match, or a geography match. Two leaders were named; they alternately chose pupils to be on their teams. In spelling, the teams lined up on opposite sides of the room, and the teacher would pronounce a word. If a member of the first team missed it, the other team would try. The one(s) who missed had to sit down. The team with the person still standing after all had missed was declared the winner.

Teams for ciphering were chosen in the same manner. Usually, one of the youngest members from each side was chosen to go to the blackboard first to solve the problem the teacher read. It might be addition, multiplication, or long or short division. The one who came up with the correct solution first won that round, and the loser had to return to his/her seat. The winner was privileged to choose the type of problem to try next. The next-youngest member of the other team was the challenger. This continued until only one member of a team remained at the blackboard and was declared the winner for his/her group.

Geography matches required that all have the same map in one of our textbooks. Sometimes we used a Kansas map, sometimes a world map. The teacher would give us the name of a city, river, or other place, and we'd have to find it. It helped, of course, to have some prior knowledge of the approximate location.

At recess, we often played Ante Over. In this outdoor game, we chose up sides; a team would stand on either side of the school building. A ball about the size of a tennis ball would be tossed over the roof as someone called, "Ante Over." If the toss was not successful, a follow-up call of, "Pig tail," was heard, and we could hear the ball bouncing back down as it rolled off the roof. When the toss was finally successful, someone on the opposing side caught the ball as it came over. Then we'd all run around the building and try to tag someone with the ball as they scrambled to exchange places with us. The person(s) tagged became members of our team. Usually, recess was over—the teacher signaled by ringing a bell—before one team succeeded in capturing the other.

In the wintertime, following a snowfall, we played Fox and Geese. Two or three pupils would find a place where no one had walked across the snow. They'd go single file, tramping out a big circle. Another circle was placed about five feet inside this one. This was then divided into four sections, pie fashion. The "fox" was chosen—someone who could run quite fast—and the rest of the pupils were geese. When he caught someone, then that person became one of the foxes. The fox had to be on the same path as the geese in order to catch one; he/she could not reach across and could only cross at the marked crossings. This continued until all the geese were caught or until the bell rang.

There were school programs. Sometimes we had a Halloween program and almost always a Christmas program. There were recitations, songs, and sometimes dialogues or short plays. Treats always followed the Christmas program. All the parents attended. The last day of school was special too. This was a neighborhood carry-in dinner. The joy of being out of school, of having an especially good dinner, and then having someone help carry your books home made this a great event. In this early day, all students owned their own books and supplies. The district bought nothing.

Transportation to and from school was thanks to old Daisy. Old Daisy, I'm sure, was the best educated horse in Jewell County! She took Archer to high school for four years, then Hattie for her four years. Grace was next. Following graduation, Grace taught at John Brown School three or four miles away and again drove Daisy to school. A gray horse named Babe made the daily trips to high school while Daisy took Grace to her teaching job. When Grace was married, Daisy resumed her former job. For two years, Addison, Marguerite, and I attended high school; and she furnished the "go power." After Addison graduated and Marguerite married, I still drove old Daisy. This old horse was on the road for at least fourteen years. Of course, Daisy was a white horse, and all her rides were bareback. I'm not sure we even owned a saddle.

Chapter 5

Chores

One day blended into the next during the school year with very little variation. There was school all day, and seldom did we have homework. We'd go directly home, change clothes, and get to work. The first job for my brother John and me (we were the youngest) was filling the woodbox for Mother's woodburning kitchen stove and for the dining room stove. We'd also have to pick up a bushel of corncobs. They were used instead of kindling to start the fires. Mother did all the bread baking and made pies and cakes. We often had a hired man to help with the fieldwork. With five to seven children, two parents, and multiple field hands, it took a lot of cooking and a lot of fuel.

Getting the wood was fun. We'd use the little wagon to haul it to the door and then carry it by the armload to the woodbox. In snowy weather, we'd pile it on our sled. But cobs? Not fun. Most of the time, we picked them up out of the pig pen. Ugh! Dad fed ears of corn to the hogs, and they stripped the kernels off. We picked up the cobs from the mess that covered every inch of the hog lot. It was especially nasty after a rain. No one in the family complained, so we learned from an early age not to complain.

Dad found it necessary and profitable to keep a dairy of some ten to twelve registered Holstein cows, but he hated the task of milking. There were no milking machines available, so the children were taught to milk as soon as they were old enough—about five years old. The beginning milker learned the skill on Midnight, a very placid old cow. We turned an orange crate upside down and slid it under the cow. Then, with a kettle on one end and the child on the other, little hands tried to master the trick of extracting the milk and directing it into the kettle. As soon as we "graduated" from Midnight, we were assigned two or three other cows to milk both night and morning.

There were stanchions for nine heads of milk cows. Usually, there were two more in the adjoining box stall. That meant sufficient work for the four younger children. Addison, my older brother, milked the ones that were most apt to kick or get a foot in the milk bucket. We had heel chains for those that were especially bad about kicking while they were being milked. This device fastened over the back of the cow's "knees" with a chain from one to the other. She couldn't kick because she could not get her feet apart. She could jump up and down.

It couldn't be all work and no play with four youngsters around. The main item of entertainment while milking, if Dad wasn't around, was squirting milk at one of the several cats that inhabited the barn. We'd aim at their mouths, and some of them learned to open up and drink while the stream of milk was available. Then the cats spent several minutes cleaning their fur. If someone started teasing one of the milkers, we knew what would come next—a stream of milk in the face.

Marguerite, my older sister, was assigned to gather the eggs. Since she was older, she was more responsible and handled them carefully. John and I often trailed after her and had great fun finding nests that the hens had hidden under the outbuildings or where they'd burrowed into the hay in the haymow.

Addison threw down the hay from the haymow to feed the livestock. The cattle were on one side of the driveway that divided the barn, and the horses, two to a stall, were on the opposite side. Mangers ran in front of the animals to contain the grain or hay. Addison was also assigned the dubious honor of cleaning out the barn. This was a daily chore with the milk cows, not quite so often with the horses. A bucket-like device suspended from a track attached to the ceiling expedited the work. The track ran from the outside door at one end of the barn down the side behind the cattle. One section of track also ran behind the horses. The excrement was scooped from the concrete gutters into the carrier, pushed along the track and out a door, and emptied onto the pile that accumulated there. This pile was later transferred to a spreader and hauled to the fields for use as fertilizer.

One of the first chores in the morning after milking and the last chore of the day was running the milk through the cream separator. This hand-operated machine separated the cream from the skim milk. The cream was stored in a five- or ten-gallon cream can and taken to town, usually on Saturday night, where it was sold, and the money was used to buy groceries. The eggs that were not used in cooking were also sold. There was usually a thirty-dozen-egg crate and at least a five-gallon can of cream sold every week. The grocery list was limited because the farm was almost self-supporting. We purchased sacks of sugar, flour, oatmeal, coffee, and sometimes macaroni. If Dad was doing the shopping, he always included a ten-cent bag of his favorite candy, peppermint pillows.

A chore we detested—reserved for the girls—always followed the washing of the breakfast dishes. This was washing the cream separator. The cream and milk left sticky deposits on the metal, so it took close attention to get it clean. There were all those disks to wash—twenty-four of them—though it seemed to be much more. They were shaped like a deep saucer with no bottom. A hole on one side permitted the transfer of the disks to a holder that looked like an oversize safety pin. On this holder, they could be washed one at a time. It took at least as long as washing the dishes.

We didn't graduate from doing chores until we graduated from high school. The quantity of livestock that Dad kept was reduced considerably as the older children grew up and left home.

Dad raised registered Holstein cattle and maintained careful records of both breeding and milk production. The horses were Percherons, the hogs were Duroc-Jersey, and the chickens were Buff Orpingtons.

We had some unforgettable animals. One Holstein bull was named Old Joe. He weighed more than a ton and had to be confined because he was so mean. He was black and white like the Holstein cows, but it is as if you took a Holstein cow and blew it up to the large bull size he was. He was huge! Holstein cows seemed docile and very approachable, but Old Joe was to be feared because of his aggressive attitude. Old Joe looking at us was enough to send us running to the house.

In order for Old Joe to get some exercise, a cable was run from the barn door to a tree about one hundred feet away. Old Joe had a ring in his nose. A chain attached to the ring was fastened to the cable, and he would prance back and forth for the full length. Once in a long while, he would get loose. We all scrambled to get inside the house when that happened. We never knew quite how Archer and Dad got him under control again. One time, Old Joe rolled Archer over a three-wire fence. Fortunately, he wasn't hurt. We were all thrilled when Dad sold Old Joe.

Dad had another bull that took such a dislike to him that Dad didn't feel safe if he were loose. One time, when he got out, Dad had to shoot him full in the face with a shotgun and blinded him in one eye. The old critter calmed down somewhat after the shooting.

Some of the older kids liked to play in the pigpens, chasing the baby pigs. One day, when Marguerite and a neighbor girl were annoying the brood, the sow chased them. The sow knocked the girl down and bit off a piece of the outside rim of her ear. That stopped all visits to the pigpens! When John and I were small, we were warned not to go near the pens because the "he-hog" would hurt us. We were told he was big and had tusks on each side of his mouth. I could envision that he must stand at least five feet tall with tusks at least eight inches long, flaring from each side of his mouth. Much later, I was very surprised to see a very ordinary-appearing boar.

Chapter 6

The Older Kids and Cars

I mentioned that each Saturday evening, we went to Formosa, and that really was an important social event for the children. Grace told of one of their trips to Formosa on a Saturday night when she was in high school. She accompanied brothers Archer and Addison. There was a long hill about a mile outside of town then called the Leydig Hill because it was adjacent to their farm. The Model T wouldn't make it up the hill and died before it reached the top. Archer was driving. He was sure that if they could push the car to the top of the hill, they would get it started as it rolled down the other side.

Grace was wearing a very special dress that night. Mother had hired Mrs. Guller to make a yellow crepe de Chine dress for Hattie to wear to the junior-senior banquet the year before. Hattie cut the dress down for Grace to wear, and she wore it that night. The skirt was full, gathered to a waistband. She and Addison pushed and pushed. As she bent over to push, Grace stepped on the hem of her skirt and ripped it away from the waistband halfway around.

The car started as Archer predicted. When they got to town, everyone except Grace went to the movie. She sat in the car all evening, contemplating her lovely yellow dress that was now in disrepair and counting the long minutes until the movie ended.

When Archer graduated from high school, he got a Scripps-Booth roadster. Now *that* was a sports car! I don't know how he happened to have it. No one else in the family *ever* had anything so fancy. As a matter of fact, Archer was the only one who had a bicycle. Maybe the idea of buying six more of anything prompted restraint on Dad's part, or maybe there were major perks with being the firstborn male child.

One Sunday afternoon in the summertime, Archer drove his convertible to Scandia with Grace as a passenger to attend a baseball game. Hawes Hill was the long incline leading to a mile of flat land adjacent to the Republican River on which Scandia was located. As they got to the foot of the hill, Archer was speeding down the dirt road like a maniac when a wheel came off the car, rolled past them, and went into a corn field. They spent all afternoon looking in the tall corn before they finally found it. The game was over by the time they found the wheel and got it back on the car.

By the time Addison was old enough to drive, my parents seldom went to town on Saturdays. Saturday was the traditional day to sell the cream and eggs and then buy groceries for the coming week. With many neighbors, it was also the time to catch up on the news, local and otherwise. They often visited until nearly midnight. I don't think Dad cared much for this activity since he avoided it whenever he could. It wasn't until much later that stores started closing at 8:30 p.m. or earlier, and the people went home earlier. Initially, the stores stayed open until everyone left town.

We had a series of Ford cars from 1913 to the 1920s and then changed to Chevrolets. The Model Ts, of course, had side curtains. Dad bought a new Plymouth in 1928.

I remember one Saturday night when Addison had driven to town with John and me in the new car. There was road construction on the highway in front of the house, so we had to go across the backyard and through the creek bed to reach the side road then go to the highway past the point of the construction work. It rained while we were in town. When we tried to drive through that creek bed at the edge of the yard, we got stuck. Addison awakened Dad and asked whether he should hitch up a team of horses to pull the car into the yard. Dad said that wouldn't be necessary because the rain was over. Unfortunately, the rain was not over. We had another storm during the night, and the water in the creek covered the motor and got inside the car, leaving a muddy deposit on the leather upholstery. Dad got the team of horses and dragged the car to town to the garage where they cleaned the motor and the interior. They must have done a good job because there were no long-term effects of the flooding.

Chapter 7

The Garden

Summertime freed us of schoolwork, but there were plenty of other things to do. First came the garden. Between our house and the schoolhouse, a creek cut off an area about a quarter acre in size. It flooded periodically, so the soil was very rich. This was our garden spot. Dad loved to garden, and we were expected to help. He planted everything according to the phases of the moon depicted in the *Farmers' Almanac.* Those crops that produced their bounty above the ground were planted in the light of the moon while root crops such as carrots, parsnips, potatoes, etc. were planted in the dark of the moon. That procedure, or something, worked successfully because his garden was always very productive.

Dad used a length of binder twine tied between stakes at each end of the patch to mark the straight rows planted with radishes, onions, lettuce, carrots, cabbage, tomatoes, peas, green beans, etc. He planted the sweet potatoes in another field with the Irish potatoes.

Keeping the garden immaculate was a family venture. Our white pony, Daisy, worked in the garden with Dad for years, and she knew exactly what was expected of her. Dad had a five-tooth cultivator that Daisy pulled up one row and down the next with Dad walking behind. She never stepped on a plant! In this way, the rows were kept clean. What about the space between the plants? That's where the children came in. We hoed between the cabbage and tomato plants, weeded with our fingers between the onions, carefully determined which of the plants were carrots or beans and which were weeds, and removed the offenders.

Planting the tomatoes and cabbage was quite a project. Dad went down the row on his knees as he set the plants in the ground, leaving a depression in the soil around each one. Usually, there was water in the creek or in the ditch adjacent to the road. Marguerite or Addison would bring the water by bucket to the area where Dad was working. Then John and I would use a tin can to dip from the bucket and pour the water carefully into the depression around each plant. The next morning, we would go to the garden and pull dry soil around each plant to keep it from crusting over where we had poured the water the night before.

Planting potatoes was a back-breaking task. The night before this job began, Dad went to the fruit cellar where the potatoes were stored. He cut the seed potatoes into pieces, making certain each section had one or more eyes. On the next day, he plowed the furrows, and we would walk down the furrow, dropping a piece of potato about every twelve inches, being very careful that each fell cut-side down. If it didn't, you would reach down and turn the piece over. Then Dad plowed the furrow shut.

As the garden grew, Mother would decide what she wanted to fix for dinner. The menu usually was chosen on the basis of the crops that were ready for harvest. We were sent to the garden to pick the peas, beans, or whatever was producing.

After we had filled our bucket and taken it to the house, it was necessary to pod the peas or string the beans. When the potatoes were large enough to use, we would dig a few by scraping the soil carefully away from the plant to find the ones large enough, being careful not to disturb the plant itself so those remaining would mature. This was a daily task until potatoes were harvested late in the summer.

About the time the potato plants reached a foot in height, the potato bugs would infest the patch. A spray did some good, but new ones were always hatching. It was a constant battle all season. Every once in a while, we were assigned the task of picking the bugs off the plants. We'd take a small bucket, walk along, and knock the bugs into the container. I think Dad then poured gasoline over the bugs. Dad laughed about the man who sent $2 to a company that guaranteed results in bug control. He received two wooden blocks with instructions to place the bug between the blocks and press firmly.

Digging the potatoes involved Dad and all the children. Each child was equipped with a bucket. Dad would hitch a team to the empty wagon, drag a plow behind, and load the kids aboard, and away we'd go to the potato patch. He left the wagon at one end of the field, hitched the team to the plow, and started down the row. The plow turned up the potatoes, and it was our job to pick them up, carry them to the wagon, empty our buckets, and go get another load. When we finished, Dad drove us back to the house, where we all helped transfer the potatoes from the wagon to the fruit cellar we called the cave.

The carrots, parsnips, onions, and turnips that were not used during the summer months were also stored in the cave for use during the winter months. For many years, we had a sizeable orchard and always had several crates of apples stored in the cave.

Mother canned beans, tomatoes, all kinds of fruit, and beef. Her canned roast beef was delicious, and the canned sausage was absolutely super. We saved the sausage for a special treat for Sunday mornings.

You can conclude from these tales that we were a well-fed family. There was always meat, potatoes, and gravy for dinner and supper along with two kinds of vegetables. Dad loved desserts, and we always had pie, cake, or canned fruit, sometimes even a combination. Ice cream was usually a special treat reserved for Sundays only. It was time-consuming to freeze ice cream, and there was seldom time to make it during the busy week.

Breakfast was always oatmeal and pancakes. Each child was expected to eat both. We seldom had eggs at mealtime since Dad did not care for them. Every child had to eat breakfast or stay home from school, and we did not want to stay home. School was easier than staying home and working. I never heard one of my brothers or sisters say, "I don't like that." We ate all kinds of food without considering any preference. All of us worked hard and ate well.

Chapter 8

Threshing Time

One of the most exciting times and one of the busiest times of the summer was wheat threshing time. When the threshers were at our place for two or three days, it meant lots and lots of work for everyone. Usually, someone in the neighborhood owned a threshing machine. For several years, it was Dad's machine that went from neighbor to neighbor, threshing wheat and oats. There was very little barley grown in our area. The threshing outfit consisted of a steam engine, a separator, and a water wagon. A long heavy belt ran from the engine to the separator to furnish power. The water wagon was just that—a wagon that actually was a tank on wheels that held water for the steam engine. It took three men for the crew to operate the machinery, one for each piece of equipment.

All the men in the neighborhood exchanged work, so essentially, the same group of men worked all season in the area until harvest was over. They would come with hayracks to pitch the bundles of shocked wheat onto the hayrack and take it to the separator. There, they would toss the bundles into the machine that separated the grain from the straw. The grain went down a tube on one side of the separator, and the straw was blown into a stack from the opposite end of the machine.

One of the younger boys usually drove the wagon loaded with grain to the farmstead where the granary was located. It was scooped into a bin by a couple of men assigned to that job, and there it was stored until sold. The sale of grain meant scooping it out again, this time into the wagon to be driven two and a half to five miles to the nearest elevator.

Counting the crew that ran the machine and all those involved with the threshing, there were often twenty to twenty-two men who would show up very, very hungry for dinner and again for supper. Only the three-man crew who ran the threshing outfit came to breakfast.

We had an icebox that provided a limited amount of storage and a limited amount of refrigeration. Usually, chicken was served at meals—for obvious reasons. Beef was expensive as well as very hard to keep fresh. Chicks were running around the yard and available for catching. Of course, they had to be dressed, the vegetables brought from the garden and prepared, and the potatoes dug. By this time of year, the early apples were ready for use, so someone was sent to the orchard to get a supply. Somehow Mother always managed. She had the reputation of being one of the best cooks in the neighborhood. She managed to have plenty of tasty food ready when the first bunch of threshers arrived at noon, ready to eat. The second group usually came at about 12:45 p.m.

With no running water in the house, how did the men clean up? Benches were set up outside the dining room door with several buckets of water, soap, washbasins, and towels. A mirror was hung on a nearby tree with a comb or two available. They did a fair job. The meal and the hour of rest revived them sufficiently to resume the hard work for another half day. Several of the men would decide to go home at suppertime to get started on their chores rather than come to the house for a meal. It was already nearing dark, and our farm was the only one in the neighborhood that had electricity.

The other time we had lots of extra men was when Dad decided it was time to fill the ice house. He had built this structure fairly close to the house. The walls were of poured concrete about ten feet high. The walls extended not more than two feet above the ground level. It was probably fifteen feet square with a shingled roof. The roof that reached close to the ground was so tempting, but we were forbidden to climb on it. Not only would we damage the roof, but we ran a great risk of getting slivers as we slid down.

Again, a crew of eight or ten neighbors with wagons would go to the appointed place—a pond or stream—where one-hundred-pound cakes of ice would be cut, loaded onto the wagons, and brought to the ice house. Dad used straw for insulation, starting with a thick layer on the floor. The flat cakes of ice were then stacked layer upon layer to within fifteen inches of the walls. Straw was packed into that space, and then another fifteen to twenty-four inches was stacked on top.

Depending on the source and the distance driven, the job was accomplished in a day, at most two days. This made possible homemade ice cream on summer Sundays! Mother had ice for the icebox too, so the time and effort to "put up ice" was definitely worthwhile.

Marguerite and I usually were assigned the job of churning butter. Sour cream was poured into the three-gallon crockery churn, the wooden dasher put in, then the lid slipped over the dasher and onto the churn. We'd stand, one on either side of the churn with one hand on the dasher, and pump the dasher up and down until the butter came. Sometimes it took an hour, sometimes only a half hour.

One hot summer day when we wanted to play outside, Mother told us it was time to churn. She took us, the churn, and the cream down to the cave where it was cool. She got it all set up for us and told us, "Now get to work." In our exasperation, we took to the task with a little too much gusto and knocked a hole in the bottom of the crockery churn. The cream ran out on the cellar floor, much to our dismay. Mother, of course, had to clean up the mess we'd made. She informed us in several different phrases that behavior in the manner we had displayed was definitely not suitable.

A description of my childhood would not be complete without telling about the huge elm tree that stood on the level land between the house and barn. It was one of the largest in the whole area.

From the trunk, one limb at a height of fifteen feet extended almost horizontally at least twenty feet. The trunk was free of branches up to this special one. Dad set a three-foot post in the ground midway between the base of the trunk and the outer reaches of that special limb. Then he climbed the tree, bent an old cultivator seat around the limb to protect it, and attached a lightweight cable to the limb in such a way that it would swivel. After embedding a heavy rod in the post, he bored a hole about three feet from the end of a two-by-twelve board some fifteen feet long and slipped it over the rod. To the other end, he attached the cable. When one would push the short end of the board near the post, the other end would revolve in a big circle. It was magic! Our own merry-go-round! We spent hours and hours every summer playing on it. It lasted as long as the tree lived, well after all the children were grown.

Chapter 9

The Day the Gypsies Came

The morning was warm with a soft breeze blowing—typical of many summer days in North Central Kansas. Addison ran into the house with exciting news: "The gypsies are coming! They just started down the hill." Since our farmstead was located on the level between two hills that were about a mile apart, we didn't know from which direction to expect them, but that didn't matter. The exciting thing was that they were actually in the neighborhood.

Back in the teens of last century, small groups of gypsies traveled in covered wagons, often with three or four horses tied to the back of the last wagon in the small caravan. An excellent campsite was provided by the rural school located just around the corner from our house, a distance of about a city block. The grounds covered about two acres, so there was grass for the horses. The cistern furnished a ready water supply, and there was outdoor plumbing available. It was typical that they would camp at the schoolhouse for a few days, maybe a week.

The band of gypsies usually consisted of four or five women, a few men, and assorted children of all ages. The women dressed in long colorful full skirts and bright peasant blouses. With their long dark hair and black eyes, they made quite a picture. If food was not freely given when requested, it was usually appropriated in some manner. The women visited farmsteads near the campsite, and the men roamed over the whole neighborhood, trading horses.

Gypsies always visited us. Late one afternoon, one of the ladies walked up to Dad, smiled, and said, "Hello, Papa. What a nice-looking papa." Then she patted Dad's stomach while chanting, "Nice belly, big belly, fat belly." She continued with, "Can I have some milk for the poor sick baby?"

We had an orchard, a large flock of chickens, and a vegetable garden, so Dad was usually generous. He hoped to satisfy their needs so they wouldn't resort to thievery.

At this time, I was five or six years old, and my brother John was almost two years younger. Mother warned us, "Now you and John stay close to the house. Don't talk to the gypsies. They steal children if they have a chance. Then you'll have to live in a covered wagon. You'll have to beg for food in order to stay alive." You can believe we took these warnings seriously. We didn't question anything, though we might have questioned how blue-eyed, blond Swedish children could ever pass as members of a gypsy band.

As I reconstruct this episode, it seemed it was again late afternoon. I had gone to the orchard to get some apples for Mother to make a pie. The henhouse was on the other side of the hedge fence from the orchard. I thought I heard the chickens making a fuss, so I slipped through the hedge to see what was causing the disturbance. I stood on tiptoes to see through the window. There stood one of the women, gathering our eggs! It frightened me. My heart raced as I turned to run, and I collided with another gypsy woman. I tore myself away from her bulky skirt and ran. I certainly didn't want to end up as a stolen child. I ran and ran until I was completely out of breath. I didn't dare turn to see how closely I was being followed. Just as I collapsed onto the ground…I awakened.

I was so terribly frightened. When I realized it was a dream, I knew I couldn't tell anyone because they'd laugh at me. I lay awake the rest of the night; taking a peek every few minutes to be sure I could still see the moonlight coming through the window, needing the assurance that I was indeed safe in my own bed. The next day, I didn't venture out of the house unless I was with one of the family. The gypsies moved on a couple of days later. Caravans of gypsies became a thing of the past when cars gained popularity as an easy mode of travel.

Chapter 10

Every Day Is a Busy Day

Monday was always washday. Upon arrival in the kitchen on Monday, we were greeted by the smell of boiling water and lye soap. Dad believed that all white clothes should be boiled with lye soap every week. He had the boiler of water heated by the time we came to breakfast.

Immediately after breakfast, he would empty the boiling water into the washing machine and start the gasoline engine. There would be a whir of belts, then the machine started agitating. Another tub was filled with water in which to rinse the clothes. The clothes then went through a wringer and were carried to the lines outside. Mother took over the project after Dad got the tubs properly filled. During most of the winter, the clothes froze stiff immediately. Late in the afternoon, they were brought into the house, and hanging the clothes on racks and chairs near the woodburning stoves would complete the drying process.

We were lucky! About 1917, Kansas Power Company ran a power line from Concordia to Mankato, right past our house. We were one of the first farm families in the country to have electricity. We had a transformer on the pole just across the road from the house. This reduced the voltage for use in the house and barn. Dad substituted an electric motor for the gasoline one attached to the washing machine as soon as one became available.

Whenever a storm came up, someone had to rush out and turn the transformer off. This required that a lever be pushed up into the Off position, and it would shut off the power to the house. We were always scared to do this, but no one was ever hurt. One night, lightning struck the transformer, and the resulting fireworks lit up the night. It looked like large blobs of burning oil that dropped to the ground from near the top of the transformer. No damage was done except to the transformer. When we knew we wouldn't get caught, we would sail the dry stalks of horseweeds so they would land across the two wires. There would be a sputter, and soon they would burn through and drop to the ground.

In the spring, Mother would start the incubator to hatch the eggs and increase the size of our flock of chickens. The largest, most perfect eggs were saved for this purpose. The incubator was about the shape and size of a card table except the tabletop of the incubator was a box about fifteen inches deep. A door at the front opened, and two flat trays slightly smaller than the tabletop could be pulled out. Mother put about one hundred eggs on each tray.

The trays were carefully placed in the incubator, the door closed, and the eggs warmed by a kerosene lamp. A thermometer was laid on the eggs. During the first week of incubation, they were kept at ninety-five degrees then at ninety degrees the second week and eighty-five degrees the third. The eggs were turned over every day. If we were very, very careful, we could help Mother with this task.

At the end of three weeks, if the lamp had not gone out and chilled the eggs, the baby chicks started pecking at the shells and soon kicked themselves free. Shortly after, they became the fluffy yellow Easter chicks one sees in pictures.

In the meantime, some of the hens had started "setting." These hens were isolated and eggs placed under them so they would hatch exactly at the same time as the incubator eggs. The old hens would have their broods increased to take care of the incubator chicks.

Some eight to twelve weeks later, the chickens would be big enough to fry, provided they had been given sufficient feed and water and no wild animals had killed them. They were also in danger of drowning in a heavy rainstorm, or a car might hit them if they wandered out to the road. When it came time to choose a bird for the family dinner, Mother and the kids would walk around the yard where chickens were always scratching. Mother would point to the biggest rooster and say, "Let's have him for dinner." Then the chase started with the dog and kids running the poor bird into a fence corner to catch him. Mother or one of the older kids would wring his neck. Mother would bring a bucket of boiling water, dunk the bird in it, and then pick him clean of his feathers. The bird was then dressed, cut up, and would appear as fried chicken an hour or two later.

One of the hazards of chicken raising was sudden thunderstorms. The mother hen would take the chickens away from the nest to find something to eat and often was quite a distance from the chicken house. When the rain started, she would settle down and spread her wings to shelter them.

When the chickens were more than two or three weeks old, she couldn't stretch far enough to protect them from the downpour.

After one of these downpours, the kids would take bushel baskets and go looking for the half-drowned chickens. We would bring them into the house, put them in a shallow cardboard box, and slip them into the barely warm oven of the cookstove until their feathers were dry. We didn't dare to close the oven door! It was smelly, but the procedure saved lots of lives.

Dad kept between 150 and 200 laying hens. We used all the eggs we needed and then sold the rest at a produce house in town when we sold the cream on Saturdays. Late in the summer or early fall, Dad would choose the largest pullets to keep for winter and sell the rest with the surplus of roosters.

The surplus cream, eggs, chickens, and garden produce kept the family solvent throughout the year. This income more than paid for groceries and incidentals. The income from crops, primarily wheat and corn, provided the working capital for the farming operations.

In addition to the chickens, we had hogs, cattle, and horses on the farm. It was seldom necessary to buy meat. Mother canned meat for use year-round. This was a real task. She didn't have a pressure cooker, so the glass jars filled with meat were placed in the washtub and set on the woodburning kitchen stove. Water was added so it reached the shoulders of the jars, and then it was boiled for the required number of hours. Mother also canned sausage in a similar way.

Nothing went to waste at our place! I thought pickled pig's feet and beef tongue were routine menu offerings. The summer kitchen was a separate building about fourteen by twenty feet and was used for storage. Whenever any of the fruits in the orchard became ripe or it was time to pick the vegetables, Dad would gather the produce and empty it on the porch floor. Mother would then proceed to handle it, meaning can, dry, or whatever was appropriate. I've watched Mother peel apples, pears, peaches, tomatoes, and other items of produce by the hour. She loved to eat the bits of fruit stuck to the pits. One day, to the amusement and amazement of everyone, Mother actually recited a risqué ditty.

> Bread and butter and apple sass,
> An old man died with a rag in his ass.
> The rag blew out, and the wind blew in…
> And the old man came to life again.

She used a word that we were not allowed to say, but she did it with such a big grin that we were all delighted! Our Mother said a forbidden word to amuse us. That was a rare event and broke the monotony for all of us.

There was an apple peeler that was put to good use as long as it was in working condition. It was a metal object fastened to the table by a clamp. The apple was skewered on three prongs, and a blade on a movable head conformed to the contour of the apple as a hand-turned wheel was rotated. Of course, the apples had to be quartered, and any peeling that the peeler had missed removed. It expedited preparation of apple butter, however. We had a cherry pitter too. It did a fair job except it would sometimes deposit a bunch of pits in the fruit instead of the discard. We had three crab apple trees, and Mother made the best spiced crab apples I've ever eaten.

Dad cured and smoked hams and bacon. For his smokehouse, he built a small rectangular structure about three by six by four feet. From the ceiling, he would hang the hams and bacon using binder twine. Some twenty feet away, he built a fire, preferably with green apple wood, and would channel smoke down a covered trench into the smokehouse. After three days of this treatment, the meat had a delicious flavor.

Dad maintained the eleven-acre orchard on the Bell Farm in addition to a smaller one on the Carlson home farm for several years. The one on the Bell Farm finally died out during the drought of the '30s. In the fall, Dad would take the back seat out of the Model T, load it with apples, and drive to one of the surrounding towns. He would come home with a salt sack full of silver dollars that he'd received when he sold the apples.

Dad was always generous with the neighbors. For many years at Christmastime, Dad butchered either beef or pork. Nearly always there was snow on the ground. Dad would hitch old Daisy to our sleigh, put the string of sleigh bells over her back, and make a Christmas morning delivery of a big parcel of fresh meat to each neighbor's house.

Dad was also generous to neighbors we didn't know so well. We had an "interesting" family who lived half a mile from us. Ike usually spoke bluntly on most any subject. One time, Onie, his wife, bought a new item in the grocery store: olives. At the table, they were passed to him, and he thought he was helping himself to small greengage plums. After a taste, he exploded, "Migod, Onie! Who peed in the plums?" This was one of Dad's favorite stories.

A family who lived a half mile the opposite direction was noted for being exceedingly close-fisted. During World War I, they would not buy bonds or make any kind of contribution to the war effort. One night, someone painted all the fence posts around their farm yellow. Almost as soon as that happened, the four family members got out there with gasoline or kerosene and cleaned off all the paint. It was removed in less than a day.

John had problems with croup when he was young. I can remember when he awakened in the night, scarcely able to breathe. He seemed to feel better in the fresh air, and I can remember sitting with him on the front porch in the middle of the night while he was recovering.

Mrs. Jack Sweet, who lived a mile north of our place, had some creative cures for ordinary ailments. Mrs. Sweet told Mother to do this for John: stand John up with his back to a door (any door would do), measure his height on the door, bore a hole in the wood at the height of his head, clip some hair from the crown of his head, and put it in the hole in the door using soap or something to make it hold there. She said, "As soon as John grows taller than that hole, he will be over his croup." Strangely, John out grew his croup about the time he grew above that spot!

Here is another cure of hers: If you cut yourself on a piece of glass or other object, rub some grease (lard or fat of any kind) on the object that caused the cut. Put the offending item on the shelf, and the cut will not become infected.

Mrs. Sweet also "manufactured" some kind of a stick salve for boils. The stick was heated, and the salve applied warm. The results were good.

Chapter 11

Tasting Soap

A common practice during pioneer days was to make one's own laundry soap. Drippings from bacon were saved. When the fat from hogs was rendered, the lard was drained off and used for cooking purposes. In our part of the country, the cracklings (the crispy part that remained) weren't considered food fit to eat, but they were saved and put in with the ingredients to make soap.

On the big day of soap making, a bonfire was lighted in the yard, and a big iron kettle hung above the flames. The fat from the various sources was dumped in along with some water and a can or two of lye. The heat from the fire made a gooey mess of this mixture. It had to be cooked to a certain consistency in order for the soap to attain the right degree of hardness when it cooled.

One day, when Grandmother Fancher was making soap, some Indians came riding past. (At various times, Pawnee, Sioux, and Cheyenne were known to be in the area.) She was certain by their actions that they meant no harm. By sign language, they indicated they wanted a taste of the White man's food that was cooking in the big pot.

What should she do? If she refused, they might become angry. The only thing to do was let them have a taste and hope it didn't make them sick. One taste was enough. They showed utter disgust at their sampling of White man's food and quietly left.

Chapter 12

Peddlers. . .and Doctors

During the late teens and early '20s, when people still relied somewhat on horses for transportation and Model Ts were becoming fairly common, there were door-to-door salesmen who traveled through our area. We could depend on the Watkins man and the Raleigh man to call on Mother every two to three months. They would arrive in a very early model van. It looked like a tin box on wheels. It was stocked with vanilla and lemon flavors, ointments, liniments, lotions, soap, pins, needles, antiseptic salves for the cattle (Bag Balm), Wasa-Tusa (for intestinal flu), St. Jacob's Oil, etc.

The salesman would carry his big heavy bag, which was well stocked with samples of the merchandise into the house, place it on the floor, and unfold it. There were hinged compartments that lifted away from the bag to make a complete display. The children were curious about the contents but trained to know that you didn't touch anything! You didn't ask questions and didn't ask for anything. Mother chose what she wished to buy with no interference unless she asked for an opinion. She kept a supply of vanilla and lemon flavoring and St Jacob's Oil.

St. Jacob's Oil was one of those magic potions that would cure almost anything. If a child had a toothache, rub on St. Jacob's Oil. If Dad had sore muscles, rub on St. Jacob's Oil. It was also good as an antiseptic for cuts, scratches, and insect bites—a sure cure for almost anything. As an adult I was curious about St. Jacob's Oil makeup. I discovered that it would probably not gain approval by the Federal Drug requirements for a safe liniment. It was made of 82 percent turpentine with trace of camphor, 10 percent ether, and 5 percent alcohol.

Denver Mud, which Dad purchased at the local store, had almost as many uses. It was always on hand and was used as a poultice on boils, infected scratches, and cuts. It "drew out the poison."

We seldom made a trip to visit the doctor and just as rarely made trips to the dentist. There were exceptions, of course. Late one afternoon, John and I got astride old Daisy to go to the pasture to bring in the cows. We were galloping along when suddenly Marguerite rode along beside us on Cupid, a feisty Shetland pony that we were keeping for a friend. Cupid nabbed at Daisy's neck. Daisy jumped sideways, and John and I kept traveling forward. We tumbled in a heap on the hard ground. I hurt my right wrist, and John had a bad bruise on his ribs. That night at supper, Dad asked me to show him my hand. I carefully lifted it up on the table with my left hand and assured him it was all right. He decided we should see the doctor. We drove the three miles to Courtland, and Dr. Snyder determined the wrist was broken, a clean break immediately above the joint. Dad held my elbow, and Doc pulled on my hand. The bone popped back into position. There were no x-rays then. He put wooden splints around my wrist, bound it up, and sent us back home. I wore a sling for six weeks. The novelty made me very popular at school. I think I was the first one who ever had to wear an arm in a sling. John had a lump on his rib for the rest of his life as a result of the bruise from Daisy's hoof.

Another doctor visit took place when Marguerite got an abscess on her jaw. It had been there long enough that Dad became worried. He didn't get that way easily. He took her to Dr. Snyder, who lanced it then put a big bandage on it. When she came home with all those wrappings, Marguerite contended she got more attention than she'd ever received in her life.

We went to the dentist only when we had a toothache…period. This may account for the fact that most of us had dental problems later. Dad had his problems too. One of his front teeth was a false one fastened to a peg. Every once in a while, it would become loose and fall out, usually at an inconvenient time. I remember one time he was in his woodworking shop. The floor was always covered with sawdust and dust. When his tooth dropped into the accumulation, we had to help him find it. It took a lot of sifting, but we were finally successful.

This lack of medical attention seemingly did not have an adverse effect on my parents. Dad lived to be eighty-two years old, and Mother survived until she had passed her ninety-second birthday.

Chapter 13

Sunday—a Day of Rest?

We almost always attended the First Methodist Church in Formosa on Sunday, often for Sunday School, and most of the time, we stayed for church. A Sunday afternoon pastime we enjoyed was riding our ponies. The Bunker family lived a half mile south of us. Shortly after dinner, Faye (a little older than me but in the same grade) and Neal (my age) would come by on their pinto ponies. We'd get old Daisy and a larger pony we called Babe and join them. John and I always went on these jaunts, and sometimes Addison accompanied us.

We'd ride a mile north to an abandoned farmhouse to explore and check to see whether a bum had been staying there. It was exciting to walk into the vacant house then up the stairs to the second floor, never knowing whether you might come face to face with a bum. Sometimes we'd ride the opposite direction to the railroad, tie the horses to a tree, and walk the rails. It seemed a delightful way to spend the time. The Bunkers had a saddle for their ponies, but we always rode bareback.

Sundays often meant family dinners. First, Sunday School, then back home to scurry around to get ready for Uncle Albert, Aunt Grace Moe (Mother's sister and her husband), and their three boys and one girl. Mit and Aunt Maggie Brown would be there too with their three girls. Maggie was Mother's cousin but was raised as her sister. This made a basic group of at least twenty people. Often, extras were invited.

Our dining room table would seat sixteen to twenty people. The grown-ups always ate first; the kids played outside until it was time for them to eat. Often, some of the favorite food was gone by the time the second group was served, but we knew better than to complain. One Sunday, we would be at Moe's, the next at Brown's. Then the Carlsons would entertain. These were all the relatives we had. We also entertained the Leonard Aspegren family quite often. They had five girls.

We particularly enjoyed visiting Aunt Maggie Brown. She would let us go upstairs to her store-room, where we could play an old-fashioned Victrola that used the heavy round cylinders. She also had a stereoscope with lots of wonderful pictures.

When we visited Aunt Grace, dinner was never ready when we arrived. Aunt Grace was usually just starting to mix up a burnt-sugar cake. That was my favorite. Often, each of the three layers would be peaked in the middle, so they didn't quite fit together like a picture. But the flavor was delicious.

Mother was an excellent cook. Her bread, pies, etc., were the best! She served whipped cream on practically everything: apple salad, apple dumplings, and apple and pumpkin pie. She even ate tomatoes with cream poured over them. She loved to eat and was plump as a girl through most of her ninety-two years.

After the various children grew up and moved away, they'd bring their children home for the Sunday dinners. Archer had six children: Hattie, five; Grace, four; Addison, one; Marguerite, three; Ruth, two; and John, two. When Mother and Dad would be surrounded by some or all of the twenty-three grandchildren, Dad would smile and whisper to Mom, "And not a dummy in the bunch."

Chapter 14

Grown Up

I completed elementary school at our country school. Near the end of the school term when I was in the eighth grade, Dad took me to Mankato on two consecutive Saturdays. It's where I wrote the county examinations. Yes, we had competency testing then! My success in passing these tests determined whether I would be permitted to enter high school. I completed them satisfactorily, so again we went to Mankato to participate in the eighth-grade graduation exercises.

For this momentous occasion, Mother had made a white organdy dress for me. It had a plain bodice with a slightly gathered skirt, and over this, I wore a modification of a pinafore. I thought it was beautiful! Mother was an expert seamstress. She made all our dresses and underclothes, everything except the underwear.

For me, high school started when I was twelve years old—in the fall of 1923. I was small of stature (almost 5') and shy beyond belief. I was afraid to speak up in class. In a special penmanship class, the instructor decided the desks were too large and that I should sit at the teacher's desk on a piano bench! To add to my embarrassment, he called me Baby Ruth!

I surprised my teachers by getting good grades on the tests that were given. They couldn't understand why I didn't participate in classroom discussions. Finally, by the time I was ready to graduate from high school, I'd gained a little self-confidence, made some friends, and generally enjoyed myself. I was the salutatorian of the class.

Growing up on a North Central Kansas farm in the early part of the last century was unique compared to modern times. We led a very sheltered life and didn't realize it. Our entire universe revolved around activities on the farm and at the country school. There was no outside influence by radio, television, questionable movies, or fast transportation. What a contrast to modern times!

There will never be another time when growing up matched my experience. I consider myself very fortunate to have grown up in the period that saw the beginning of radio, television, airmail, scheduled airlines, jet engines, x-rays, medications like penicillin, and computers, the first man to walk on the moon, astronauts, atomic technology, and much more.

And it looks like the best is yet to come!

Maggie Bell

Victor Emil Carlson

Maggie and Victor Carlson
Wedding, 1896

Left to right: Hattie, William Bell
(grandfather, Maggie's father), Archer

Mr. and Mrs. Karl Johan Carlson
(Victor's parents)

Front, Archer, Maggie, Victor, John; *back,* Ruth,
Hattie, Addison, Marguerite, Grace

Fiftieth Wedding Anniversary
Front, Victor, Maggie; *middle,* Hattie, Grace, Marguerite, Ruth;
back, Archer, Addison, John

Ruth, about twenty years old

Ruth, about eighty years old

About the Author

Ruth Carlson Wareham graduated from Formosa, Kansas High School at the age of sixteen. By passing a test, she was certified to teach in a one-room school, which she did for two years. In the spring of her second year, two women from the Wichita, Kansas Business College recruited her for their program. She knew she did not want to go on teaching, so she paid the women a $100 down payment on her schooling. She did this because she knew her father would not want her to go on her own to Wichita but was too frugal for her to waste the $100 payment. She was correct. Her father did object but could not allow her to waste $100.

While in school, she stayed with a family for room and board. She did housework and took care of the children when not attending class. After finishing the program, she eloped and married Paul Victor (called Bill) Metz from Mankato, Kansas. They had two children: Victor Clare in 1936 and Linda Louise in 1939. In 1944, Bill volunteered to serve in the Navy. While traveling on the train for his first leave, he died of scarlet fever. Ruth went to work for the Soil Conservation Service in Mankato to support her family. When the Soil Conservation Service office in Mankato was transferred to Manhattan, Kansas, she moved the family there in 1952.

After being a widow for twenty-seven years, she married Ralph I. Wareham, and they enjoyed fifteen years together before he died. They enjoyed traveling and made some remarkable trips. In addition to traditional travel targets in Europe and Hawaii, they traveled to the North Pole, Afghanistan, Arabia, Australia, China, Crete, India, Thailand, and Tibet. With Linda and her family, she traveled to the Holy Land and Egypt. In Egypt, in sight of the pyramids, she rode a camel and remarked, "It neck-reins just like a horse!"

Ruth's retirement hobbies included learning to oil paint and becoming an excellent artist, embroidering six quilts for children and grandchildren, making glass-bead flower arrangements, teaching English as a second language, working with the Manhattan Historic Society, playing bridge, and reading to a blind woman. She also enjoyed staying in touch with her siblings and wrote them weekly. With her love and appreciation of her family, she wrote these stories in 1985, when she was seventy-three.

CPSIA information can be obtained
at www.ICGtesting.com
Printed in the USA
LVHW071158230822
726655LV00007B/163

9 781639 858279

Staying at the Table

BEING THE CHURCH WE SAY WE ARE

TERRI HORD OWENS

chalice PRESS

Print: 9780827212961

EPUB: 9780827212978

EPDF: 9780827212985

ChalicePress.com

Contents

Foreword   v

Introduction   ix

Everything Begins with God   1

Let's Start with Limitless Love   19

Imagine with Me   31

Let's Be the Church We Say We Are   47

Staying at the Table   71

Changing the Narrative   87

I Want a Church …   97

Foreword

By William J. Barber II

When Pope Francis published his encyclical *Laudato Si'*, I was grateful to have the opportunity not only to read a church leader's letter to his global communion but also to travel to the Vatican and respond to his message as a sibling from another branch of the global family of faith. That journey concretized for me the importance of a genre of writing that is not well-known outside the Roman Catholic Church—the encyclical letter.

The encyclical is a pastoral letter written to a particular communion with the intention of being overheard. As the "servant of servants," the pope listens to the bishops, who listen to the pastors, who listen to the people in parishes all around the world. Because he bears the burden of all those stories, he must be disciplined in his commitment to pray for the church and listen to God. This isn't a job that anyone could do on his or her own. But the office of pope is where the gifts of many come together to trust the Spirit to guide the church.

When the pope writes an encyclical, it says to the people in every parish what he has discerned about where God is leading the church. But it isn't just sent to the parishes. It is published for everyone to read and respond to. I made the journey to Rome, even though I am not Roman Catholic, because the pope understands listening to those outside his authority to be an important part of the process of writing an encyclical.

The small book you're holding is an encyclical letter in its own right. Terri Hord Owens is my dear sister and my general minister in the Christian Church (Disciples of Christ). She is the first African American woman elected to lead a denomination in the United

States—a denomination that is predominantly White. In her office as general minister, she has listened closely, discerned carefully, and reimagined church processes, and she has offered a vision for our future. Like the pope, she has done this with the support of many. But she has embraced the full responsibility of the office, in obedience to her vocation and for the sake of the world.

Staying at the Table is an extension of that faithful work. Before she was elected, Terri was clear about her diagnosis that we are "biblically illiterate and spiritually dry." This pastoral insight was not a condemnation of any person, but an insight that the church has failed in its call to help people learn to read the Bible and practice their faith in ways that sustain the life of the spirit. As a teacher rooted in the Stone–Campbell tradition and her own pastoral experience, Terri offers practical tools for Bible study and spiritual practice. But this pastoral guidance is offered in the context of a vision for the life of vibrant faith communities and institutions that serve the life of the world.

As in Christian worship, the table is central—both as practice and as metaphor—to this book. Importantly, our attention is drawn to God's table, at which we are all guests. Because we do not have the power or authority to exclude anyone whom God has welcomed, staying at this table is an invitation to learn new ways of being together that can bring good news to our neighborhoods, to our nation, and to the world.

At a moment when so many people have been disappointed by Christianity and confidence in churches is low, publishing an encyclical letter is a bold and audacious act. I have heard our general minister share the message she shares in this book at our denominational meetings and in ecumenical gatherings with other church leaders. It is an important message in those spaces. But why publish this pastoral message for anyone and everyone to read? What is the public purpose of an encyclical letter?

Maybe the "open table" at the heart of this book's message isn't possible to conceive or proclaim apart from publishing its message for all to hear. As general minister, the author is not only pastor to her flock; she is also a prophet to the world, called to tell a story that challenges the stories that divide us and prop up so much injustice. Whether our neighbors share our tradition or not, they are in desperate need of this kind of story and the solidarity it can inspire. May *Staying at the Table* be a catalyst for conversation about how the story at the heart of the Christian story can resonate with others to bring life and hope to our world.

Introduction

"Everything begins with what we believe about God." "We don't need more words or a new mantra or program. We have wonderful words. We need to be the church we say we are." I preach some version of these messages wherever I go. If you are looking for a four-point formula to spur church growth or a methodological template to follow, this is not the book for you. If you are looking to better understand how we work together to build a world that is possible because of Jesus' transformative love, I believe you will find inspiration in what follows.

Just as our physical health requires commitment to diet and exercise, so our spiritual health requires spiritual practice and biblical literacy. Mainline Christianity suffers from a pervasive absence of both. Spiritually dry people are not equipped to be the kind of followers of Christ who can model the radical love and hospitality that God commands. We will not even grasp the breadth and transformative nature of God's revelation of love through Jesus unless we are seeking always to know God both in our own practice and through the sacred text. Once we have even a glimpse of understanding God's limitless love, we can dare to follow Jesus' teaching and we can have confidence in the God who is able to do far beyond all that we can ask or imagine.

The Christian denomination I currently lead, the Christian Church (Disciples of Christ), honors the importance of the Lord's supper and the new covenant that Jesus establishes at the Lord's table. We say that we "welcome all to the Lord's Table as God has welcomed us." If God is indeed a God of limitless love, we must embrace the inherent dignity and value of all whom God has created. We must recognize that the Lord's table is not just about the meal we share; it is about the community of God that we create together. We can come to the table eager to share in the fruits of its love and peace and committed to ensuring that everyone finds that same love and peace.

We do not have the right to restrict access to the meal we celebrate as the Lord's supper, but we must also understand that we do not have the right to restrict access to the community of God. We are called, rather, to ensure that there is always room for at least one more. The limitless God cannot be subject to the limits of our own prejudices and biases. We do not have the right to exclude one another's humanity, and we do not have the right to ignore the oppression of our neighbor.

And if we accept that all are welcome, that all have worth and dignity, then we can commit to the hard work of *staying at the table*. We are called not just to eat the meal; we are called to do the work that will usher in the kingdom of God that Jesus always talked about. Staying at the table requires that we truly love God *and* love our neighbor, recognizing that her welfare is our welfare. Staying at the table means that our own seats there require facing truths that are thorny and uncomfortable.

When people ask me what I am doing about evangelism, I tell them the best way to tell people about Jesus is to fight for their flourishing, to ensure that all have what they need to live and to feed their families, that all have access to affordable and excellent health care, that all live in housing that is safe and affordable. Jesus was crucified and rose again, yes, Hallelujah! But we are the people of the resurrection, called to stay at the table even when it is hard, even when we disagree. We are so firmly grounded in this radical welcome at the table of the Lord that it is clearly articulated in our Disciples of Christ Identity Statement:

> We are Disciples of Christ, a movement for wholeness in a fragmented world. As part of the one Body of Christ, we welcome all to the Lord's table as God has welcomed us.[1]

Within these pages, I share my vision for the theological grounding I believe makes it possible to stay at the table and be the church we

---

[1] "Disciples: Who We Are," Disciples.org, accessed May 19, 2025, https://disciples.org/our-identity/.

say we are. If we believe that God is a God of limitless love, then we fully embrace the humanity in each one. We stand in the confidence of this limitless God who is able to do far beyond all we can ask or imagine (Ephesians 3:20). If we begin with the foundation of God's love, then there are certain roads we simply cannot take. And if we are committed to reflecting God's limitless love, the covenant that Jesus established at the table of the Lord must be reflected in the community we build together.

It is not enough to invite others to share a meal of bread and juice. We must invite all—no matter the extent of our difference or division—to be co-laborers as we work for the society the Hebrew prophets wrote would be possible because of the Messiah. We do so because every time we share that meal, we are called to remember the covenant Jesus established on the night when he was betrayed. We are not called to build buildings or to have long lists of names on membership lists. We are called to bring about the kin[g]dom of God here on earth because Jesus has come and shown us how to live and how to love. From this foundation of faith and confidence in God can come an openness to imagination that is not afraid to do and be all that Jesus taught.

I also share the work that my denomination has done to live into being the church we say we are. It is certainly not the only way, but I hope it provides insights and an example of how one part of the body of Christ is wrestling not only with our heritage, but with how we live into the gospel in ways that are relevant for our time. Certainly, this is my perspective, but I hope that Disciples of Christ might gain a clearer understanding of the vision, created alongside so many other faithful ones as we seek to imagine a new church for this new world.

We have declared for decades that one of our priorities is to be an anti-racist/pro-reconciling church. We are a covenantal church with a congregational polity. Each congregation calls its own pastors and may own its own building or other resources. In our highest decision-making body, the General Assembly, every congregation has voting delegates. We are the only mainline denomination that provides such a voice.

Our middle judicatory, known as regions, are led by regional ministers. These ministers are accountable to a regional board and serve as a resource for congregations and pastors, *not* as an ecclesial form of authority. We also have general ministries that serve the entire denomination. These ministries have separate executives, each accountable to the ministry's board. All of these regions and general ministries are accountable to a General Board, a smaller body charged by the General Assembly, to do work on its behalf. The General Assembly is at the top of our structure, *not* the General Board.

Congregations are the lifeblood of our body. My role as head of communion carries with it no direct operational authority except for the small staff who serve in the Office of the General Minister and President. Covenant for us is certainly a "want to" proposition, not a "have to" commitment. In addition, we are a binational church, with congregations in the United States and Canada.

In this context, we have made the choice to lift up the radical welcome of the Lord's table and to be an anti-racist church. We are also committed to leadership development, to starting new faith communities as we imagine who we must be as a new church for a new world.

Early in my tenure as General Minister and President, I engaged consultants to ask the questions: Do our congregations understand who we are? Are we communicating well about our identity to ourselves? To others? The answer has come back: Disciples know these statements. My conclusion was that we do not need new words or mantras. We simply need to be the church we say we are.

We have recently made significant changes to our governance that are not about moving chess pieces or even about propping up our institutions; rather, they are about seeking to ensure that our processes reflect our commitment to who we say we are and to the value that every voice is welcome. The ever-increasing cost of travel has created barriers for too many of our congregations, limiting their participation in the meetings of the General Assembly. New rules will allow for annual digital gatherings and provide more time for education, discussion, and discernment, not just voting up or down on an agenda item. We cannot stay at a table to which we have little access. We cannot stay at the table when we do not fully understand what the basis of the discussion is. And we cannot faithfully support or oppose anything unless we are in dialogue with one another.

Ensuring that all of our congregations can engage in our governance reminds us all of the power of each community. We are examining ourselves, region by region, to reimagine the narrative into which we have been living, recognizing that we must create together a preferred narrative of our shared future to build an environment that enables wide participation. We have asked ourselves, "What do you want someone to know, experience, and feel when they are part of one of our congregations?" We are asking hard questions so that we can name and face the problems, and together we are learning how to stay at the table to create a church that can choose to address these problems.

None of this is easy or comfortable. All of it involves navigating disagreement and bridging wide chasms of division and polarization. But all of it is possible because we serve a God who is able to do far beyond all we can imagine. We must stand on that confidence. All along the way, this means we also participate in shaping the laws and policies that govern our societies. Using a lens of love, we must commit to choosing to make our society a safe and just world for everyone. If we really believe that God is love, the lens of love will shape our choices every step of the way. We cannot be afraid, for the very viability of our message depends on our commitment to this radical love.

Imagine with me, if you will, a God who is able to do far beyond all we can ask or even imagine. Imagine with me, if you will, a church in which love and hospitality know no limits. Imagine, if you will, a society in which followers of Jesus live as he did, spending time in prayer and scripture, focusing on building the kin[g]dom of God, in which justice is available to all—because that is how God's love is made visible. Imagine, if you will, a church that challenges any system of oppression or exclusion because it is inconsistent with what God tells us God desires.

Human systems can indeed be subject to God's love if we decide to stay at the table and commit to love. We can indeed learn how to discuss, debate, question, and come to consensus and solution. This is only possible by the power of God's spirit working within us. It is only possible when we presume charity, when we presume that we are operating from love and not from an intentional desire to harm or hurt one another. Staying at the table so that we can build a community that will hold together after we eat the bread and drink from the cup is necessary in order to bring about the kin[g]dom of God here on earth. It is in such a community that we can be witnesses to Christ and reflections of God's limitless love.

As the great theologian and biblical scholar Walter Brueggemann said, humans can implement anything. We must not only imagine, he said; we must get inside God's imagination. Only by inhabiting the limitless nature of God can we envision the world as it ought to be. More words reflect only our human ability to engineer ideas and processes. We do not need new slogans, strategies, or methodologies. We simply need to be the church we say we are, building a just world in which all have enough. In doing so, we bear powerful witness to God's limitless love for all.

Everything Begins with God

Now to him who by the power at work within us is able to accomplish abundantly far more than all we can ask or imagine, to him be glory in the church and in Christ Jesus to all generations, forever and ever. Amen. (Ephesians 3:20–21)

I remember learning the "omni" words—omnipotent, omniscient, omnipresent—in Sunday school. I learned that God was all-powerful, all-knowing, and always present. The God I learned about created all that I could see and even what I could not see. God was bigger and stronger than anything I could understand. God knew everything, far more than I could ever hope to know. And no matter what, God was always present with me. God so loved the world, I learned in John 3:16. This amazing God was also a God of limitless love.

With a childlike faith, I accepted this understanding. When I was taught that God loved the world so much that God sent God's Son, Jesus, to reconcile the world to God, it made sense that this awesome and loving God would do something like that, and I made my confession of Jesus as Lord and Savior when I was six years old. It is certainly true that part of my confidence in my belief system came from my confidence and trust in my pastor—my grandfather. But it is also true that, decades later, having lived a lot of life and experienced a lot of joy and pain, that understanding of God has been my bedrock. I still believe that God is all-knowing, all-powerful, and ever-present and that God loves with a limitless love.

Everything we believe or understand about our faith begins with what we believe about God. What we believe about God determines our understanding of our relationship with all creation and all humanity. What we believe about God determines how we understand and articulate who Jesus is and how we understand his teachings. What we believe about God determines how we understand our own place in creation, and how we understand God shapes our perspectives and guides our actions.

What we believe about God can determine how we engage with others and the reasons we hold for that engagement. If we are grounded in how God sees others and the world around us, we can choose to align our understanding with God's. We cannot begin to imagine how to be in relationship with others unless we understand God's nature and how God sees those relationships. More importantly, we must conclude that our own criteria for these relationships must always yield to how God defines such relationships.

In order to be the church we say we are—and to be committed to staying at the table—we need to really believe and trust in who God says God is. I believe that God is unconditional and limitless love. If that is what I believe, I must always make choices that are consistent with that belief. Believing that God is unconditional and limitless love helps me to center and understand who Jesus is, why he came, and what he taught. Jesus is the incarnation of God's limitless love. Without that understanding, we actually limit who God is. No one can limit God, and I reject any theology that allows for humanly derived limitations on whom or how God loves.

The proclamation of God's limitless love is the message at the heart of the good news of Jesus Christ. Jesus is the incarnation of that love, and through Jesus that love is revealed. In Jesus' teachings and example, we learn more about how to reflect that love in the world. Staying at the table is a call, first, to claim our place as part of the covenant that Jesus established at the Lord's table; second, to recognize that it is the Lord's table, not ours, and we are called to honor God's invitiation and welcome; and, finally, to understand that part of the covenantal relationship with God and one another is to stay at the table.

We stay despite disagreement, confusion, even anger and disappointment, for it is only by staying at the table that we can truly live into this covenant with God and one another. It is only by staying that we can bear witness to the power of believing so much in the love of God that we are willing to lay aside our human differences. We stay so that the world sees that, because of this limitless love, we are able to walk together even when we disagree. It is no easy task, and it is possible only because of God's limitless love and our commitment to staying. If we do not affirm God's limitless love, we open up cracks in our understanding that can be undermined by human bias, weakness, and conflict.

Despite our own human bias and whatever we may think of our human brilliance, we do not get to decide that God's love, power, and ability are limited for anyone or any group. The moment we begin to delineate limits or exclusions to God's love, authority, or ability, God is no longer God. God cannot be subject to humanly defined limitations. This important premise is at the heart of this book and at the heart of the message I find myself preaching in every sermon.

In 2025, my denomination's General Assembly theme is based on Ephesians 3:20–21: "Beyond." Our hope is to remind ourselves that God is the one who is able to do far beyond all we can ask or think. The words of the King James translation of the Bible are especially powerful: "Now unto him that is able to do exceedingly abundantly above all that we ask or think, according to the power that worketh in us." When we remember that the God we serve, the God who sent Jesus, is able to do beyond anything we can imagine, we move forward with the confidence that only comes from this limitless God.

How do we really know who God is? How do we really know God's nature? As Christians, the authoritative source for knowing about God is the Bible. I do not speak of the Bible in a literal or dogmatic sense; I speak of it as the authoritative text for the Christian faith. I believe that each one of us has access to God through the power of that text, enabled and guided by the Holy Spirit. My tradition claims that, although we may disagree on scriptural interpretation, we nevertheless agree that we each have the authority, even the responsibility, to engage the biblical text for ourselves. Through the prophets and the gospels, we learn about the God who has moved throughout human history to establish love, justice, and peace.

The prophets were often called upon to remind the people of God's great power, often in the midst of oppression and disappointment. The teachings of Jesus call us to live out the commandment to love God and our neighbor. The gospel writers share the stories of Jesus' ministry and give us a window into how we might live as God intended. The writers of the epistles share inspiration and encouragement to the earliest Christians.

The God who created all things must be understood as being beyond our full comprehension. The God of covenant must be understood as one who will not fail to keep faith with God's people. The God of love must be understood to be a God of limitless love, whose love is never beyond the reach of any of us, whose love can never be denied by one of us to any of us. If there is a guiding interpretative lens, it must be a lens of love, the love that the Creator has for all creation, abundant without limits. I once heard someone say that if you are interpreting the scriptures to mean that God hates, rejects, or demeans anyone, you are reading it wrong.

The words of scripture inform and ground our understanding of who God is. As you read and study the scriptures in the following pages, I pray they will become a touchstone for you, a way to bolster your own faith, and words that will inspire and comfort you as you seek to be a faithful follower of Jesus, a reflection of God's love and glory. These passages are often where we find insights into who God has declared that God is, through the words of the prophets or in the hymns of praise or lament.

I am always mindful that even the language of scripture is, at best, an attempt to use our limited human tongues to describe and convey the fullness of who God is. There are no words sufficient, no words eloquent enough, no phrases powerful enough to truly convey God in God's complete fullness ... but these words do give us some important insights to guide our understanding. Below are some examples of powerful scriptures that tell us who God is and share attributes of the Holy.

According to Deuteronomy 10, Moses spent forty days on Mt. Sinai, receiving the law we know as the Ten Commandments for the second time. He had destroyed the first tablets in anger at the Israelites' disobedience. As Moses reminds the people of his first forty-day visit to Mount Sinai, he reminds them of the great commandment to love and serve the Lord first and foremost, and he declares the greatness of God:

> *For the Lord your God is God of gods and Lord of lords, the great God, mighty and awesome, who is not partial and takes no bribe, who executes justice for the orphan and the widow, and who loves the strangers, providing them food and clothing. You shall also love the stranger, for you were strangers in the land of Egypt. You shall fear the Lord your God; him you shall serve; to him you shall hold fast; and by his name you shall swear. He is your praise; he is your God who has done for you these great and awesome things that your own eyes have seen.* (Deuteronomy 10:17–21)

In these verses, we hear God described as "great," "mighty and awesome." We hear, not for the last or only time, that God executes justice and care for widows, orphans, and strangers. Just as God loves the strangers, the people are commanded to love them, for the Israelites "were strangers in the land of Egypt." We are called to love and worship God because God has done great things for us, and in response to that love we are also called to love. We are also called to love and worship God simply because there is none who is like God. God is simply beyond all other power, all other love.

It is important to claim that understanding as the foundation for our faith and as the grounding of the work we do as followers of Jesus. If we can claim this limitless God of love, power, and strength, we can then stand in that confidence when life's challenges come our way. It is our confidence that God is beyond our understanding, that God is able to do far beyond anything that we can think or imagine, that allows us to trust God all along the way.

David was just a shepherd boy, the youngest son of Jesse. He spent his days in the fields with his father's sheep, caring for them and singing worship to God. After a visit from the prophet Samuel, he became God's chosen king of Israel. A hallmark of his life is worship and praise to God, writing the vast majority of the psalms in the book of Psalms. As part of the books of history in the Hebrew Bible/Old Testament that give an account of David's reign, he declares in 1 Chronicles 16:34:

> O give thanks to the LORD, for he is good, for his steadfast love endures forever.

That refrain, the "steadfast love" of God, is echoed by Nehemiah. The prophet who led the rebuilding of the walls of Jerusalem also refers to the "steadfast love of God in Nehemiah 9:32 and 13:22. The psalms declare over and over the steadfast love of God, but one of my favorites is Psalms 100:5:

> For the LORD is good; his steadfast love endures forever and his faithfulness to all generations.

The prophet Jeremiah declares that there are no limits to God's abilities or power:

> Ah Lord GOD! It is you who made the heavens and the earth by your great power and by your outstretched arm! Nothing is too hard for you. (Jeremiah 32:17)

One of the most rewarding ministries I have served in was the new membership development ministry at a church while I was in divinity school. This church was, by today's measures, a "mega-church," and I taught several classes of forty to forty-five new members for several weeks. The majority of the students were newly baptized, but the classes also included new members who had transferred membership from other congregations, denominations, and traditions. One of my goals was always to establish a habit of prayer and Bible study as important spiritual disciplines. Start with five minutes a day, I would say, and keep building as you feel comfortable. The testimonies that came back were amazing. Students would often ask, "Where do I start reading the Bible?" Some would suggest the gospels, particularly the gospel of John, but I also suggested the psalms.

In the psalms, we find an expression of every human emotion, so many situations and conditions with which we can relate. We also learn in the psalms that we can wrestle with God. We can indeed shake our fist at God, be angry, and express our disappointment and our frustrations. The psalms show us it is possible to express all those emotions and yet never really lose a posture of praise, for every expression of anger, pain, and doubt ends with a declaration of who God is.

Even psalms of lament close with that affirmation of praise. David, the ancient king of Israel—a man God described as a man "after his [God's] own heart" (1 Samuel 13:14)—understood that, no matter what would come his way, God was yet God. Through David, many of the psalms give us language when our own feelings and frustrations threaten to chip away at our faith in and remembrance of who God is.

The psalms provide us with some of the most powerful testimonies to God's greatness. We hear of the awesome nature of God's creative power and majesty, God's provision and security, God's protection of the vulnerable, and God's ability to defeat the enemies of God's people. I invite you to read these texts aloud and allow them to resonate in your heart and mind.

> *O Lord, our Sovereign, how majestic is your name in all the earth! You have set your glory above the heavens. Out of the mouths of babes and infants you have founded a bulwark because of your foes, to silence the enemy and the avenger. When I look at your heavens, the work of your fingers, the moon and the stars that you have established; what are humans that you are mindful of them, mortals that you care for them?* (Psalms 8:1–4)

> *The earth is the Lord's and all that is in it, the world, and those who live in it, for he has founded it on the seas and established it on the rivers.* (Psalms 24:1–2)

Make a joyful noise to God, all the earth; sing the glory of his name; give to him glorious praise. Say to God, "How awesome are your deeds! Because of your great power, your enemies cringe before you. All the earth worships you; they sing praises to you, sing praises to your name." Selah. (Psalms 66:1–4)

Let the heavens praise your wonders, O Lord, your faithfulness in the assembly of the holy ones. For who in the skies can be compared to the Lord? Who among the heavenly beings is like the Lord, a God feared in the council of the holy ones, great and awesome above all who are around him? O Lord God of hosts, who is as mighty as you, O Lord? Your faithfulness surrounds you. (Psalms 89:5–8)

The Lord is king; he is robed in majesty; the Lord is robed; he is girded with strength. He has established the world; it shall never be moved; your throne is established from of old; you are from everlasting. (Psalms 93:1–2)

For the Lord is a great God and a great King above all gods. In his hand are the depths of the earth; the heights of the mountains are his also. The sea is his, for he made it, and the dry land, which his hands have formed. O come, let us worship and bow down; let us kneel before the Lord, our Maker! For he is our God, and we are the people of his pasture and the sheep of his hand. (Psalms 95:3–7a)

For great is the Lord and greatly to be praised; he is to be revered above all gods. For all the gods of the peoples are idols, but the Lord made the heavens. Honor and majesty are before him; strength and beauty are in his sanctuary. (Psalms 96:4–6)

Bless the Lord, O my soul. O Lord my God, you are very great. You are clothed with honor and majesty, wrapped in light as with a garment. You stretch out the heavens like a tent; you set the beams of your chambers on the waters; you make the clouds your chariot; you ride on the wings of the wind; you make the winds your messengers, fire and flame your ministers. You set the earth on its foundations, so that it shall never be shaken. (Psalms 104:1–5)

Great is the Lord and greatly to be praised; his greatness is unsearchable. (Psalms 145:3)

The Lord is gracious and merciful, slow to anger and abounding in steadfast love. The Lord is good to all, and his compassion is over all that he has made. (Psalms 145:8–9)

Great is our Lord and abundant in power; his understanding is beyond measure. (Psalms 147:5)

We also learn much about the greatness, goodness, and nature of God from the words of the Hebrew prophets. The prophets were tasked with speaking God's truth to the people in the midst of difficulty or their own disobedience, admonishing them to heed God's warnings and avoid God's consequences. However, the prophets always reminded the people of who God is, reminding them not only of God's power and greatness but of God's goodness and love, of God's faithfulness to them, and of the promises God had made. The prophets called the people to remember who God is, instilling hope in the call to remembrance and praise.

Isaiah was one such prophet. Renowned theologian Walter Brueggemann argues that Isaiah never gives up on God's promise of newness, grounding the argument in God's nature and determination, not in the merit of the people of Israel.[2] Isaiah is familiar to most Christians in large part because of the many texts Christians interpret as references to the Messiah. Scholars have delineated the book into two and sometimes three sections: First Isaiah (chapters 1–39), Deutero-Isaiah (chapters 40–66), and even Third Isaiah, which further divides the last few chapters.

Israel's history includes multiple periods of being conquered by foreign nations and even being carried away into Babylon, living for generations in exile. Isaiah is the prophet who emerges to speak to Israel on behalf of God during this time of exile. It is Isaiah's task to help keep alive the hope of the promise and covenant that God gave through David—that the throne of Israel would never leave the house

---

[2] Walter Brueggemann, *Isaiah Volume 1: Isaiah 1-39* (Louisville: Westminster John Knox Press, 1998), 9.

of David and that a Messiah would come to deliver Israel. As you might imagine, after multiple traumatic periods of oppression and exile, the people need hope.

Biblical scholars claim that the first forty chapters of Isaiah represent Isaiah's care for this people in exile, whereas the second half of the book (known as Deutero-Isaiah, meaning "second Isaiah") represents a new hope articulated that brings the people back to God's promises. Journeying through these pre-exilic/exile/post-exilic phases of Israel's journey, Brueggemann argues that the God of the "new thing" in Deutero-Isaiah is established by the God of the first several chapters.[3] Christians have adopted much of this theology as we have sought to understand this God of great love who sent Jesus as the incarnation of God's love.

One of my favorite texts in Isaiah establishes the holiness of the presence of God.

> *In the year that King Uzziah died, I saw the Lord sitting on a throne, high and lofty, and the hem of his robe filled the temple. Seraphs were in attendance above him; each had six wings: with two they covered their faces, and with two they covered their feet, and with two they flew. And one called to another and said, "Holy, holy, holy is the Lord of hosts; the whole earth is full of his glory."* (Isaiah 6:1–3)

In the Black church tradition from which I come, all you need to do is say those first few words, *"In the year that King Uzziah died,"* and you will hear amens and shouts of praise and see hands lifted in response. You might even see a period of musical praise as the congregation allows itself to enter into the image of holy worship. This depiction of the holy presence of God establishes for many the sacred nature of God's presence. God's presence is awe-inspiring, it is high and lifted up, and it fills the temple—it is everywhere. In the presence of such a holy presence, one is profoundly humbled, and all that can be said is "Holy, holy, holy." (Isaiah 6:3).

---

[3] Ibid.

As a preface to Isaiah's own call story, these verses offer an image of a God whose powerful presence causes any who stand there to feel unworthy. Isaiah expresses his own unworthiness, and this holy God who has asked "Who will go for me?" reaches forth to blot out any sin and guilt with a hot coal on Isaiah's lips. This great and merciful God does not diminish God's power in the moment, but that power is complemented by grace and love. One can say yes to this God, who becomes accessible and yet remains ineffable.

No doubt many clergy resonate with Isaiah's call story. We have felt unworthy, unsuitable, ill-prepared, and in many cases unwilling to acknowledge the call, let alone accept it. But God also calls each one of us, whether or not it is a call to vocational ministry. There are gifts given in abundance to bear witness to God's limitless love wherever and however we serve. For those who have accepted a call to vocational ministry, there has been some sense of the greatness of God and the overwhelming nature of God's love and acceptance that we read in Isaiah's story.

I know laypersons who have felt this same powerful tug on their spirits, feeling God's call to serve in new and different ways and to make deeper commitments. They, too, experience this sense of the greatness and overwhelming nature of God's love and acceptance. It is this understanding of God's power filled with grace and love that grounds our understanding of the gospel of Jesus. God *must* be this holy and this overwhelmingly powerful to be filled with the limitless love that caused God to seek reconciliation with all of creation.

This holy, almighty God is thus established in the first few chapters of Isaiah. In Deutero-Isaiah (Isaiah 40–66), Isaiah reminds the people of that God whose power and love they had already come to know and trust.

> *Have you not known? Have you not heard? The Lord is the everlasting God, the Creator of the ends of the earth. He does not faint or grow weary; his understanding is unsearchable. He gives power to the faint and strengthens the powerless. Even youths will faint and be weary, and the young will fall exhausted, but those*

who wait for the Lord shall renew their strength; they shall mount
up with wings like eagles; they shall run and not be weary; they
shall walk and not faint. (Isaiah 40:28–31)

Isaiah brings the people back to their earlier knowing: that God was with them, that God could accomplish anything on their behalf. No matter how they had failed, even though they had experienced the trauma of exile and removal from the land they had known, they could trust that God would continue to be God and that God would move in history on their behalf. God would continue to be God!

Through the prophet Isaiah, God speaks to the people to counter any reluctance or uncertainty they might have. Surely, we too are in need of this assurance in our times of difficulty and trauma. If we can trust in this understanding of God as being beyond anything we know or are, we can lean into a faith that counts on God being who God says God is.

> *For my thoughts are not your thoughts,*
>   *nor are your ways my ways, says the Lord.*
> *For as the heavens are higher than the earth,*
>   *so are my ways higher than your ways*
>   *and my thoughts than your thoughts.* (Isaiah 55:8–9)

The prophet Jeremiah lived in the period following the destruction of the Jerusalem temple in 587 BCE. As in Isaiah, the understanding of God that Jeremiah lifts up for the people is one that depends on God's keeping of the covenantal promises, regardless of the Israelites' failure to do so. Above all, the message is that there is no one like God, none like YHWH. This assurance of the prophet comes even as the people know that the very place where they believed God dwelt had been destroyed. They would need to distinguish God from other deities that were still physically defined by places or icons.

> *Their idols are like scarecrows in a cucumber field, and they*
> *cannot speak; they have to be carried, for they cannot walk. Do*
> *not be afraid of them, for they cannot do evil, nor is it in them*
> *to do good.* (Jeremiah 10:5)

By continuing to trust that God was still the all-powerful God even without a temple, a new theological understanding was being developed. This theological shift is consistent with the message of Deutero-Isaiah: No matter what we face, God is yet God. Our God is with us.

> *There is none like you, O Lord; you are great, and your name is great in might. Who would not fear you, O King of the nations? For that is your due; among all the wise ones of the nations and in all their kingdoms there is no one like you.* (Jeremiah 10:6–7)

In the New Testament, we continue to find witnesses to God's greatness and power. Jesus reminds his disciples that he on his own can do nothing. He is sent to do God's will and to show the people the nature of God.

> *Jesus said to them, "Very truly, I tell you, the Son can do nothing on his own but only what he sees the Father doing, for whatever the Father does, the Son does likewise."* (John 5:19)

> *"I can do nothing on my own. As I hear, I judge, and my judgment is just because I seek to do not my own will but the will of him who sent me."* (John 5:30)

Jesus' teaching about love is his central definition of God's greatness and goodness. We will explore that more fully in the next chapter, "Let's Start with Limitless Love".

Grounded in this faith of his ancestors, the apostle Paul will later share with the Ephesians that God is able to do far beyond anything they could ask or think of. Paul is familiar with the writings of the prophets and the history of his people; this understanding of God was part of his training (Philippians 3:5). His conversion experience led him to reembrace it more fully, almost as though he himself had been in exile from that knowledge, having persecuted Christians as though God would have him do it. He finds his own salvation in embracing the God of limitless love as revealed in Jesus Christ, and he ministers to a Gentile world about this goodness and abundant love of God.

Paul offers what I believe is a profound testimony to the greatness and goodness of God by comparing God to human attributes and accomplishments. Paul's own background, he claims, has given him serious credibility in the Jewish tradition. Yet all the training, education, and status is nothing in comparison to the newness he has found in Christ. Just as Jesus pointed his followers to God and did not seek to elevate himself, Paul reminds the church at Corinth that Jesus' power comes from God. Not only that, but none of us is greater than God, and any attempt to compare ourselves to God is a vain and foolish exercise.

> *Where is the one who is wise? Where is the scholar? Where is the debater of this age? Has not God made foolish the wisdom of the world? For since, in the wisdom of God, the world did not know God through wisdom, God decided, through the foolishness of the proclamation, to save those who believe. For Jews ask for signs and Greeks desire wisdom, but we proclaim Christ crucified, a stumbling block to Jews and foolishness to gentiles, but to those who are the called, both Jews and Greeks, Christ the power of God and the wisdom of God.* **For God's foolishness is wiser than human wisdom, and God's weakness is stronger than human strength***.*
>
> *Consider your own call, brothers and sisters: not many of you were wise by human standards, not many were powerful, not many were of noble birth. But God chose what is foolish in the world to shame the wise; God chose what is weak in the world to shame the strong; God chose what is low and despised in the world, things that are not, to abolish things that are, so that no one might boast in the presence of God. In contrast, God is why you are in Christ Jesus, who became for us wisdom from God, and righteousness and sanctification and redemption, in order that, as it is written, "Let the one who boasts, boast in the Lord."*
> (1 Corinthians 1:20–31; emphasis added)

Paul lived in a time when Greek and Roman culture was seen as the epitome of civilized society. The ancient Greeks, in particular, elevated the search for the highest knowledge as a sign of human excellence and superiority. Your human value was tied to how educated you were in matters of philosophy, history, the arts—all defined by the dominant Greek culture. Those who reached what they considered a higher level of understanding were considered wiser and superior to others.

But Paul declares that God is higher and greater than anything humans can lay claim to. God's foolishness, we read in 1 Corinthians 1:20–31, is wiser than human wisdom. In my family and culture, we use the term "foolishness" to refer to things that are silly or funny, things we are simply "clowning around" with—not things we would take seriously. If, in fact, God has foolishness, foolishness as we might understand it as humans, then even that foolishness is wiser than human wisdom. And in our embrace of the fact that God is simply beyond our understanding, we can allow that to exist as part of our reality. God is more. God is so much more.

The gospel is grounded in the understanding of God's ineffable greatness, God's unbounded wisdom, and God's limitless love. Indeed, there is a comfort in allowing ourselves to rest in that understanding. All of our theological claims and constructs are simply our limited human attempts to make sense of something that is beyond us. We have only our limited human vocabulary to describe and define our experiences.

Many of us like to pride ourselves in our profound theological insights. We can and should be inspired by theologians and scholars whose language about God gives us an entry point into deeper understanding and firmer faith. But we must be mindful that *all of us* are theologians. Theology is simply our way of making sense of what we believe about God. We all have this ability and, indeed, we all have this responsibility to give an account of what we believe … although we may disagree in how we articulate it.

The Christian Church (Disciples of Christ) has its roots in the claim that, no matter the various divisions based on doctrine or creed that might arise,

> [T]he church of Christ upon earth is essentially, intentionally, and constitutionally one; consisting of all those in every place that profess their faith in Christ and obedience to him in all things according to the scriptures, of groups who called themselves Christian.[4]

My tradition names the unity of all Christians as the "polar star" of our church. We have no "test of fellowship," no rules that determine whether you are "in" or "out." If we accept the radical nature of God's limitless love, we can then accept that none of us can declare that my truth is greater than your truth, and that participation in the wider ministry of Christ cannot be limited to those who agree with me on various ideas or beliefs. Our primary governance document, *The Design of the Christian Church (Disciples of Christ)*, includes only this confession in its Preamble: "We confess that Jesus in the Christ, the Son of the living God, and proclaim him Lord and Savior of the world."[5]

This unity we seek is grounded in the radical welcome to the table of the Lord, a welcome that must extend to active participation in the community of God. Staying at the table means you allow that not everyone will, or must, agree with you on everything. A simple confession of Jesus as the Christ is our common confession.

My deep commitment to the idea that we must not only welcome all to the table but *stay at the table* is grounded in this radical, inclusive welcome. I want every person to be assured of God's love, and I want our church—no matter the congregation, no matter where it is located—to be a place where everyone can truly experience the love that is inclusive, radical, and never-wavering.

Augustine—the noted theologian known as Bishop of Hippo in the fifth century—is considered one of the most important theologians of early Christianity. He confessed that he was pretty much a "party animal" before confessing Christ and becoming a monk. One of his

---

[4] Thomas Campbell, *Declaration and Address of the Christian Association in Washington* (1809).

[5] "The Design of the Christian Church (Disciples of Christ)," Disciples.org, accessed May 21, 2025, https://disciples.org/our-identity/the-design/.

most familiar quotes is this: "For you have made us for yourself, and our heart is restless until it rests in you."[6]

This prayer has always evoked for me a sense of the love God has toward us and God's deep desire to be in relationship with God's creation. For so many who are searching for a sense of belonging, purpose, and a way to make sense of this human journey, it is comforting and inspiring to believe that God has created us with relationship in mind and that we are not wholly ourselves unless we are connected to this Creator God. We cannot lean only on our own constructs; we must lean into the longing for a God who is far more than we can understand. I think it is dangerous to be so certain of what we know that we reduce God to a theological argument. If we are hesitant to stand on the limitless nature of God, I daresay it is because we are reluctant to acknowledge that there are some things we simply cannot fully comprehend.

As we seek to live into Christian unity, the first thing we should be able to agree on is the limitless nature of God's love; the greatness and magnitude of God's power and compassion; and the acknowledgment that we, as God's creation, can in no way limit who God is, what God can do, or how God may choose to move in human history. The very moment that we, in our human arrogance, attempt to limit God, God is no longer God. I don't want a God who is bound by someone else's constraints and limited understanding or biases. A God of no limits must be understood through a lens sharpened by the belief that God's love includes all, that God is inclusive and not exclusive, expansive and not reductionist. *The Design of the Christian Church (Disciples of Christ)* ends with the benediction and affirmation offered in Ephesians 3:20–21. It is, I believe, a common belief that we can share about who God is that will supercede any doctrinal or dogmatic disagreements. Whether we disagree on a wide range of doctrinal positions, surely we can agree about the magnitude of the Creator God. Everything we do must begin with this affirmation of who God is. It is that faith that nourishes the power at work within us.

---

[6] *Confessions,* trans. Henry Chadwick (Oxford University Press, 2008), bk. 1, chap. 1, 3.

Now to him who by the power at work within us is able to accomplish abundantly far more than all we can ask or imagine, to him be glory in the church and in Christ Jesus to all generations, forever and ever. Amen. (Ephesians 3:20–21)

REFLECTION

1. What are your favorite biblical texts that remind you of the greatness of God? What songs do you enjoy that lift up the limitless nature of God?

2. How would you describe God? Are there words from pastors, theologians, scholars, or others that you find meaningful?

3. How does reading the biblical texts bolster your understanding of God? What texts can you call to mind that inspire and comfort you?

4. Have you ever had an experience of God's acting in your life when words fail you in describing it? Have you ever tried to share a testimony or share a joy about what God has done in your life? What kinds of language do you use for God?

5. How might Christian unity be grounded in a simple understanding of who God is?

Let's Start with Limitless Love

Perhaps no other word in any language carries so much meaning, is laden with so many connotations, and yet is the most powerful concept in human existence than *love*. We are taught from an early age how to say "I love you" to parents, grandparents, and family.

In our adolescence, we struggle with what love really means, and we fret over whether someone who has caught our eye feels the same way about us. All of us can identify with the way we felt when we "fell in love" for the first time. The popular music industry leverages our feelings to make money for many artists. We hang on the words of love songs when we are young because we do not always have the right words ourselves to express what we feel. Even now, hearing those songs takes us back to a time and place when we had fallen for someone or were suffering from unrequited love. Few of us escape heartbreak in our teenage years, and that heartbreak can distort our view of love if the wounds never heal.

Maybe you have been blessed to find a lifelong love. If so, you and your partner have, no doubt, had a journey as you have sought to understand how love is lived each day, realizing that this kind of loving relationship is a choice you make every day, placing the utmost trust and depositing your own truths into the sanctity of the relationship. When marriages fail, it is hard to reclaim that security once trust has been broken.

For those who have been blessed to have a relationship with parents that is nurturing and loving, love *from* your parents is the first comforting assumption that they are there, that they provide for you and support you. As we grow older, our need to establish our own sense of self causes us to question what we've been taught, what we have experienced, and how our parents have shown their love to us. We want that love to be given as we need to be loved or it isn't real to us.

For others, perhaps that kind of nurturing presence was provided by a grandparent, aunt, uncle, or other caregiver. Our human development is shaped by that nurture, by that kind of love and support that seeks not only to meet our human needs but to give us wings to be all that God has called us to be. For many of us, our friends are often those persons who see us deeply, respect us, and appreciate us despite our flaws. They are the place where we can deposit our own truths and feel secure in the safety of such a relationship.

Speaking as a parent and now as a grandparent, I'll admit that my understanding of what it means to love a child or grandchildren is visceral. For my son and my grandson, there is nothing I would not do or sacrifice to ensure their safety and well-being. I was blessed to have the deep love of two parents who, although they ultimately divorced, gave my siblings and me a firm foundation in life. Our mother's devotion to us was complete and unconditional, and we were committed to ensuring that we returned that love in providing for her in her final years. Having seen that kind of motherly love, it is what I hope my son and grandson will remember of me. My father, a retired Black studies college professor, showed us love by ensuring that we knew our history as young Black people, requiring us to read a book per week and shaping our sense of ourselves as confident and proud to be Black.

And yet we struggle with these images of love because far too many of us have not known the warmth of such love being shared by a partner, parents, or friends. It is often the case that people resist the idea of loving one another as God has loved us simply because they cannot believe that anyone could love them in such a way. Unfortunately, we have limited our understandings and definitions of love to that which we encounter in our human relationships. We want to feel good about it and feel good about the person we love. Our human understanding of love is limited because we humans are limited. We need all kinds of coaching and support to be the loving persons we want to be, even for those we care deeply about.

For Christians—and, indeed, people of nearly all religious traditions—love is the central value. Jesus affirms God's commandments to love God and to love our neighbor.

> *When the Pharisees heard that he had silenced the Sadducees, they gathered together, and one of them, an expert in the law, asked him a question to test him. "Teacher, which commandment in the law is the greatest?" He said to him, "'You shall love the Lord your God with all your heart and with all your soul and with all your mind.'" This is the greatest and first commandment. And a second is like it: "'You shall love your neighbor as yourself.'" On these two commandments hang all the Law and the Prophets."*
> (Matthew 22:34–40)

Some of us were raised with the understanding of a God who loves us and wants us to flourish. For others, the idea of someone who loves without limits is beyond our human ability to comprehend. It is hard to imagine that God loves you fully and completely if you have never experienced anything close to unconditional love. There are many who reject the idea of God as mother or father because their own experiences with those persons in their lives have not been positive. What a complicated relationship so many of us have with the idea and experience of love in our lives. Unexplored, unprocessed, and buried trauma often keep us from embracing the very idea of love to which God calls us.

And loving our neighbor? Are we really supposed to "love" those who disagree with us, those who disrespect us and our humanity, those who align with policies and ideologies we find harmful to ourselves and our society? Are we to love those we absolutely despise? What's more, we're commanded to love our neighbor *as ourselves*. That's a tall order in part because we often have a difficult time loving and honoring ourselves.

Many Christians have been taught that to love is to deny oneself, to put others first, to make sacrifices for others before attending to your own needs. In a world where caregivers—be they health care professionals, pastors, teachers, or others—are exhorted to take time for themselves, we still struggle with the idea that, unless we take care of ourselves physically and emotionally, we have little to share with those who need such care from us. To love your neighbor as yourself is only possible if you have learned to value your own flourishing. To love your neighbor as yourself is to want for them what you want for yourself.

We all want health, safe and affordable housing, food security, an education that does not depend on our zip code, respect for our culture and traditions from those outside those traditions, the freedom to worship as we choose, the right to determine how we will identify, the right to love as we love, to marry whom we wish to marry. If you love yourself, you want rest and reward for the honest work that allows you to provide for your family. If you love your neighbor, you want exactly that for your neighbor too.

The love that God commands does not depend on how we feel or on our circumstances. The Greek definitions of different kinds of love can help us to a certain extent. *Agape* (ἀγάπ), *philia* (φιλία), and *eros* (ἔρως) are often used to help us understand the distinction between various types of love we have for a partner or friend and the kind of love that God shows toward us and that we are to show to fellow human beings. *Eros* is the kind of passionate love one feels for a partner. *Philia* is the kind of love we have for close friends, the kind of "brotherly love" that Jesus is said to have for his disciples (John 20:2) and for his friend Lazarus (John 11:3). *Agape* is the kind of love we are to have toward all of humanity, even when we disagree.

Agape is best understood as the kind of limitless, unconditional love that God the Creator has for all of God's creation. It is the kind of love that we are called to try to give, to follow the example of Jesus as the Incarnate Son of God, the expression and revelation of God's *agape* love for humanity. This kind of love is not based on any criteria or reciprocity. This kind of love is what we do simply because God has commanded us to do so. Our sincere efforts to love in this way are the closest we come to God's limitless love and to God's very essence, which scripture tells us is love.

Beloved, let us love one another, because love is from God; everyone who loves is born of God and knows God. Whoever does not love does not know God, for God is love. God's love was revealed among us in this way: God sent his only Son into the world so that we might live through him. In this is love, not that we loved God but that he loved us and sent his Son to be the atoning sacrifice for our sins. Beloved, since God loved us so much, we also ought to love one another. No one has ever seen God; if we love one another, God abides in us, and his love is perfected in us.

By this we know that we abide in him and he in us, because he has given us of his Spirit. And we have seen and do testify that the Father has sent his Son as the Savior of the world. God abides in those who confess that Jesus is the Son of God, and they abide in God. So we have known and believe the love that God has for us. God is love, and those who abide in love abide in God, and God abides in them. Love has been perfected among us in this: that we may have boldness on the day of judgment, because as he is, so are we in this world. There is no fear in love, but perfect love casts out fear; for fear has to do with punishment, and whoever fears has not reached perfection in love. We love because he first loved us. Those who say, "I love God," and hate a brother or sister are liars, for those who do not love a brother or sister, whom they have seen, cannot love God, whom they have not seen. The commandment we have from him is this: those who love God must love their brothers and sisters also. (1 John 4:7–21)

We are to love simply because God has loved us so much. Because of our conflation of the different understandings of love, we often think we are supposed to feel good about or toward all those we engage. We think that we cannot love those with whom we disagree or those who hold opinions that do us harm or who take action to diminish our humanity because we are offended or angered by what they do or say.

Too many believe that their own biases and prejudices can trump this commandment to love. They may argue that those who have offended others are not worthy of love or respect. This is the hard task of those who follow Jesus: to love as God has loved us. Period. It is not about how we feel but about our call to bear witness to the limitless love of God. We are called not to be doormats but to show dignity in how we disagree. We are called to show respect for the humanity of all—even those with whom we have strong differences. That is not to say we cannot critique or disagree. It is to say that love requires that we respect others, that we value others as part of God's creation, whether we agree or not, whether we like them or not. It is just that simple, even as it is just that hard to do. There are no circumstances that release us from the command to love.

When I was in the second grade, I had a minor disagreement with one of my close friends. I was upset that this little girl was ignoring me, and so I returned her treatment. We were huffing and puffing and trying to ignore each other in the reading circle. After reading period, our teacher asked us to step outside into the hall. "You do not have to be best friends," she said, "but you must respect each other while you are here at school." Those words have stayed with me.

As the former pastor of my home church, Dr. Tom Benjamin, always says: "We do not have to agree, but I must respect you and you must respect me."

Like you, I have often been outraged because of some offense from another person, some act of betrayal—being lied about, watching people operate with underhanded treachery, witnessing the overt injustices in our society against women, Black people, immigrants, members of the LGBTQ+ community, and those who are poor or low-wealth. As a Black woman, I have lived in a world where I have not always been welcome or safe in many places. I was born just before the civil rights movement resulted in important laws that guaranteed me the right to vote. I and one of my siblings have been the victims of racialized physical violence. My grandfather and father faced death threats because of their work in civil rights in southern Indiana. But the most important lesson I learned from the civil rights movement was insistence on the philosophy of nonviolence.

In 1995, John Dear interviewed Congressman John Lewis of Georgia about his views on love as Christian. The interview was subsequently published in *Sojourners* magazine after Lewis' death. The late congressman shared why his commitment to nonviolence was so absolute:

> At an early age, I came to appreciate the philosophy and discipline of Christian love. So, I view nonviolence as Christian love in action. It is a part of my faith; it is believing that love is the most powerful force in the universe. And somehow, someway, you have to live it.[7]

Lewis was the victim of a brutal attack on the demonstrators who planned to march from Selma to Montgomery, Alabama, in 1965. At the time, Lewis was a part of the Student Non-violent Coordinating Committee (SNCC) and a young leader in the movement. He was leading the marchers as they began to cross the Edmund Pettus Bridge. When the crowd refused to turn around under threat from the local police, they were brutally attacked, with Lewis suffering a massive head injury. The day became known as "Bloody Sunday."

When Lewis speaks of the discipline of love, he does so as one who has understood the power of that discipline to disarm the hatred he faced. He is not condoning the evil or hatred, but he strongly affirms the humanity of those who are purveyors of evil against humanity. His response was not to attack, even as he was being beaten. How, we might ask, can you actually love like that? Lewis said:

> *You have to arrive at the point as believers in the Christian faith that in every human being there is a spark of divinity. Every human personality is something sacred, something special.* We don't have a right as another person, or as a nation, to destroy that spark of divinity, that spark of humanity, that is made and created in the image of God.[8] (emphasis added)

---

[7] John Dear, "Read John Lewis on the Discipline of Christian Love," *Sojourners,* accessed May 21, 2025, https://sojo.net/articles/read-john-lewis-discipline-christian-love.

[8] *Ibid.*

As we explore what it means to "stay at the table," I believe this core understanding is key: we don't have a right to harm, disrespect, or damage those whom God has created. This is what it means to love your neighbor as yourself. The Christian Church (Disciples of Christ) declares in its identity statement:

> We are Disciples of Christ, a movement for wholeness in a fragmented world. As part of the one Body of Christ, we welcome all to the Lord's Table as God has welcomed us.

At the heart of our theology of the Lord's table is the firm understanding that all are welcome. We have no authority to limit or bar another from the table. It is, after all. not our table—it is the Lord's. Just as we are clear about the broad inclusive nature of our understanding of the table, we must be just as firm about the broad inclusive nature of the love Jesus teaches us to have both for God and for our neighbor. We don't have the right to decide whom God loves, and so we cannot be selective about who we love. We simply don't have the right.

Our world has become increasingly polarized over the last decade. Many believe they should be free not only to do or believe as they wish but to discriminate or oppress those who disagree with them. And many who are the most insistent upon the denigration of those who disagree with them claim to be followers of Jesus. Christian denominations have even split over varying interpretations of scripture, doctrines, and dogma that flow from those variations.

The tradition of the Christian Church (Disciples of Christ) was established with the firm belief that we cannot judge the veracity or efficacy of another's doctrine. We confess that Jesus is the Christ, the Son of the living God, and proclaim him Lord and Savior of the world. It is love for one another that should keep us from the presumption to ascribe valuations to what others believe. The key metric is whether we are obedient Jesus' command to love God and to love neighbor. We are never in a right position with God when we construct a doctrine that would deny any whom God has created the freedom not just to worship as they choose but to hold doctrinal opinions that differ from ours. Our work is to persuade all that any doctrine or dogma that is rooted in the love of God and neighbor cannot be one that diminishes the humanity of another. Again, we do not have the right to limit the family of God based on our inherently limited human understandings.

One of the biggest challenges denominations are facing is schism over doctrinal positions. The inclusion of LGBTQ+ persons has long been a conversation that has resulted in deep division, including splits within denominations. In many cases, I have seen congregations choose to disaffiliate with their denomination because the church or church leader made a formal statement they did not agree with. My denomination does not have a faith statement that requires adherence in a binding way. "Statements of witness" or "resolutions" are our way of allowing the voices of those who gather as our General Assembly to speak *to* the church, but not *for* the church. These statements or by the denomination or its leader are not binding on any person or congregation. For example, although many of our churches support ordination of LGBTQ+ persons, no one is required to do so, nor is any congregation required to call an LGBTQ+ person as a pastor or a member of their staff. And yet several congregations have chosen to disaffiliate because of the General Assembly's position.

I have also seen congregations choose to disaffiliate because they thought the denomination was focusing too much on anti-racism work. Getting the report when a congregation chooses to disaffiliate is always a heavy moment, and I'm grateful there haven't been any more than there have been. My regret is that somehow we have not yet learned to live into what it really means to stay at the table. It is precisely in these moments when we disagree that our commitment to the gospel is most powerful. When we stay at the table, we are saying that the gospel is more important than whether you are right or I am wrong on any particular matter. It goes back to remembering that none of us has the right to decide whom God loves or welcomes.

What does this have to do with love? God's love is not limited to those who agree or are obedient. There may be consequences for all of us in choosing not to walk the way of God or being disobedient to what we believe is right, but God never removes us from God's arc of love. There is never a condition that would take God's love from us. For any one of us to decide who is not welcome—or who to exclude because of what we believe is sinful—means that we have chosen to limit who God is and whom God loves. I'll say it again: *We do not have that right.* At the height of any disagreement, love and respect for human dignity must always prevail. We cannot do that on our own. That is why we need spiritual grounding and biblical foundations that leverage the lens of God's limitless love. I cannot claim to be a follower of Christ unless I am obedient to his commandment to love as he loves us.

Quite often during Jesus' ministry, he was asked questions that were intended to be "gotcha" questions. He was challenged on some interpretation of Jewish law or scripture and asked about it when he said or did something that others thought was blasphemous against Jewish law and tradition. Jesus' answers were also firmly grounded in scripture, but they were also grounded using a lens that insisted on the recognition of God's love for all. The response of the religious leaders was often one of shock or disagreement.

Quite often, however, even Jesus' disciples found it hard to hear his answers. Such an occasion occurs in John 6:60, after the multiplication of the loaves and fishes, when Jesus is teaching in the synagogue in Capernaum. He begins to share with the disciples that he is the bread of life and that those who believed in him would eat his flesh and drink his blood. "When many of his disciples heard it, they said, "'*This teaching is difficult; who can accept it?*'" (John 6:60) I love the King James Version translation of the disciples' response: "*This is a hard saying; who can hear it?*" (John 6:60 KJV) "Hard sayings" are truths we find hard to accept and do, even when we fully understand that they are right. Hard, yes, but necessary if we are truly committed to bearing witness to God's limitless love.

In 2016, following the tragic shooting at the Pulse nightclub in Orlando, Florida, I wrote and posted a reflection on social media. I repost the reflection often to remind myself and others that, as John Lewis said, we don't have the right to destroy that spark of divinity that was made in the image of God. This is what I wrote:

> If we begin with love, there are only certain roads available to us. Love cannot lead to fear, hate, destruction, condemnation, exclusion, discrimination, and bigotry. Love can only lead to respect, honor, dignity, compassion, and inclusion. As Jesus taught, everyone will know if we are his disciples if we have love for one another. Every religious tradition has a version of the Golden Rule, which calls for loving and honoring others as we love and honor ourselves. We have to find a way to love and respect one another even when we disagree. You do not have the right to destroy me because you disagree with me. Love cannot take you down that road. It is anathema to love to sanction destruction.[9]

REFLECTION

1. How have your own life experiences shaped your understanding of the meaning of love? Have you experienced disappointment from family or other relationships that have resulted in cynicism about the nature of love?

2. If God commands us to love God and to love neighbor as we love ourselves, what would you say are the necessary conditions to live into this commandment?

3. What does this verse mean to you: "Whoever does not love does not know God, for God is love." (1 John 4:8)

4. Would you be able to commit to nonviolence in the way that John Lewis and others in the civil rights movement did? Why or why not?

5. What relevance do you think the scriptures in this chapter have for Christians today?

---

[9] Terri Hord Owens, Facebook post, June 13, 2016.

6. What other scriptures can you share that help us understand God's nature and the importance of love for Christians?

7. What do you think about congregations that choose to leave a denomination because they disagree with a particular statement or policy? Or about people who choose to leave a church because they disagree? What guides your thinking in these matters? How might staying at the table produce a different kind of witness to the gospel?

Imagine with Me

When I was first called to lead the Christian Church (Disciples of Christ) as general minister and president, I spent time with trusted colleagues, mentors, and friends to discuss how I believed God was calling the church to serve in the future. After my first year in office, I gathered a small group to spend time in retreat with me for a few days. One of the pivotal questions that was asked of me was, "Terri, what excites you or inspires you in what you have seen across the church thus far?" My response was, "I am excited by congregations who dare to imagine that church and discipleship could be different than it has been."

I had in my mind a visit to a congregation that had sold a grand, prominent building in the heart of downtown in their mid-sized city. That congregation was worshiping at a family fitness center, with their sound equipment, chairs, and other worship supplies being stored in cabinets and closets. They set up round tables each week in the back of a rather large multipurpose room, set up coffee and pastries in the back, and allowed people to remain at those tables during worship or to move forward to sit in the rows of chairs. A model of their planned new building was on a table, a tangible image of the imagination that drew them forward into their future.

They had abandoned prime downtown real estate; to some, it felt like they were sacrificing visibility. But their building had become an albatross, an inflexible structure that would be quite costly to retrofit for the needs of their current congregation and the ministry they envisioned they could have. They changed their name (gasp!), their location (more gasps!), and their modes of worship (even more gasps!). They began to focus more on how they would reach out to address the issues facing their community—not just the area around their old building, but the entire community in which they lived.

They were growing, and they were close to completing the building of that new facility. I felt an energy in their fellowship and their worship that, quite frankly, was uncommon in the places I had visited elsewhere. They weren't looking at rows of empty seats, and they weren't fighting the time-honored battles of pews vs. chairs, "contemporary" vs. "traditional" worship styles, or any of the other elements of church life and mission that so many books have been written about. They hadn't settled in on a single answer or formula.

Instead, they were seeking to know God better, to follow Jesus more, and their spiritual growth was yielding space for what had once been considered impossible. They found their church to be just as relevant and inspiring as their own way of being, for they understood that God was calling them forward to be a new church for a new world. They knew that the future did not have to, nor could it, look exactly like the past to be relevant and promising.

At our retreat, my group of interlocutors sensed my excitement about this example, and the next morning, one of them mentioned Walter Brueggemann's *The Prophetic Imagination*[10] and shared some quotes and scripture that undergirded all that I had shared. Brueggemann's seminal text is now over fifty years old, and as I reread through the pages, I felt a new sense of energetic kinship with the book that I had read as a divinity school student. Now more than twenty years on from those days, I find Brueggemann's words speaking to my current ministry context in a powerful way. Since that time of retreat, I have read and reread *The Prophetic Imagination,* along with other Brueggemann works in which he has continued to reflect on what he means by *prophetic* and *imagination*.

So many were asking me, "Terri, what will your theme and program be?" I had resisted the notion that what we needed was a four-bullet program. Having established close communication with my living

---

[10] Walter Brueggemann, *The Prophetic Imagination: 40th Anniversary Edition* (Minneapolis: Fortress Press, 2018).

predecessors, they affirmed my sense that something more, something new was needed, not just my version of what had previously been done. I believed that what the church needed was more than just a formula or the newest concept offered by church growth consultants. I had named my priorities of spiritual growth and biblical literacy as the foundation for all that we needed to do and be as church. Reading Brueggemann's work, my travels to be with congregations, and meetings with leaders at the general and regional levels had all reinforced my sense of what God was saying. We had to learn to imagine before we could implement any change, and that imagination must be fueled by and grounded in an understanding of the limitless nature of God. As Brueggemann wrote:

> The prophet engages in futuring fantasy. The prophet does not ask if the vision can be implemented, for questions of implementation are of no consequence until the vision can be imagined. The imagination must come before the implementation. Our culture is competent to implement almost anything and to imagine almost nothing. The same royal consciousness that make it possible to implement anything and everything is the one that shrinks imagination because imagination is a danger. Thus every totalitarian regime is frightened of the artist. It is the vocation of the prophet to keep alive the ministry of imagination, to keep on conjuring and proposing futures alternative to the single one the king wants to urge as the only thinkable one.[11]

In his 2012 work, *The Practice of Prophetic Imagination*, Brueggemann outlined this thesis as he reflected on his initial thinking on just what prophetic imagination is:

> [P]rophetic imagination is an attempt to imagine the world as though YHWH—the creator of the world, the deliverer of Israel, the Father of our Lord Jesus Christ whom we Christians

---

[11] Ibid., 78

come to name as Father, Son, and Spirit—were a real character and an effective agent in the world.[12]

Referring to what he wrote, Brueggemann continued in the second edition of that book:

> The key term in my thesis is "imagine," that is to utter, entertain, describe and construe a world other than the one that is manifest in front of us, for that present world is readily and commonly taken without such agency or character for YHWH. Thus the offer of prophetic imagination is one that contradicts the taken-for-granted world around us.[13]

What indeed could the world be if we as the church imagined what the world could be because of Christ? Isn't this what all the Hebrew prophets had imagined when they spoke of the coming Messiah? Is this not the kindom of God that Jesus taught and preached, a world in which God's love and the example of Christ changed things and was the central character of the world? Could we not participate with God in changing the world if we could imagine together?

The Governance Committee of our General Board has the responsibility to submit recommendations useful for the development of the life, mission, work, and organization of Christian Church (Disciples of Christ). In September 2019, the committee met in retreat and was invited to prayerfully consider how God was leading. The Preamble to *The Design* was read, and the group called our attention to several scriptures that each member felt were illuminating. The words in the Preamble that caught our attention and lit a fire within us were these:

> We rejoice in God,
> maker of heaven and earth,
> and in God's covenant of love
> which binds us to God and to one another.

---

[12] Walter Brueggemann, *The Practice of Prophetic Imagination: Preaching an Emancipatory Word* (Minneapolis: Fortress Press, 2012), 2.

[13] Ibid., 17

We emerged from the retreat agreeing that one of the most important issues facing us was the lack of connection of so many congregations to both the regional and general (churchwide) expressions of the denomination. In order to even imagine and live into that future vision, we needed to reclaim our covenantal life and ensure that our processes and structure enabled that life more effectively.

At the 2020 meeting of the General Board of the church, I presented my annual "State of the Church" address. Along with lifting highlights of ministry across the denomination, I always tried to name challenges. In the two previous years, I had shared the objectives I had set with the moderator team (our chair and vice-chairs of the General Assembly). This year, I wanted to cast a vision for the importance of the power of imagination for the church, and the role of a prophetic imagination as we sought to continue to be a relevant witness to the gospel of Jesus Christ.

Sharing Brueggemann's words, I stressed that the role of the prophet— indeed, the role of the church—is not just to critique "the empire" or things as they are, but to develop a vision of what the alternate society could in fact look like. I told the General Board that we must imagine who we must be as a new church for a new world. I framed this invitation to imagination in what we needed to do going forward; I also gave examples of how we were already doing some of this across the church. We needed courage to change, to let go of what wasn't working. We needed to give ourselves permission to change, and we needed to walk in the freedom to change. We needed to be free from the fear of what we would happen if we let go, if we stepped forward into a future that we could dare to imagine. We were already committed to think, pray, study, and worship together. I reminded the General Board that our covenantal life together as church is grounded in scriptural literacy, theological engagement, spiritual formation and growth, and our grounding in an inclusive welcome at the table. We needed to reclaim that heritage, to revive our commitment to spiritual practice and engagement with the scriptures.

The Governance Committee shared the reflections that had been the core part of the retreat and led the General Board in discussion. The conversations were generative, and the feedback we received let us know that this grounding in covenant and reinvigorating our spiritual foundation was going to be the key. This workshop material would become the foundation for what is now "Covenant Conversations," a five-week video-based study for small groups and individuals, made available in a digital format.[14]

I left that board meeting excited and energized by the response to the work on covenant and the call to prophetic imagination. The church had sponsored theological writing on covenant in past years—but now, rather than an institutional focus, we were calling on a theological understanding that would ground us as we imagined together how best to live into that covenantal life. We have a congregational polity that I once heard described as "the most congregational of all the congregationalists." With limited authority and accountability across our life together, we would need to truly reclaim a theological understanding of covenant that centered on God's commandment to love and on our covenant with God, which Jesus established at the Lord's table.

That covenant is the basis for our very existence: we believe that *all* are welcome at the Lord's table, that *no one* can determine who is worthy, and that there can be *no* "tests of fellowship" to determine who can be in that sweet communion and fellowship with God and God's people. As for me, I wanted the church to embrace the welcome at the table as more than just a welcome to a meal; I believe it is a metaphor for the whole community of humanity, the community of God to which Jesus offers an invitation through the covenant he established when he instituted the Lord's supper.

That General Board meeting happened in mid-February 2020. Three weeks later, the world was in lockdown because of the COVID-19 global pandemic. The new world I had called us to imagine had landed in our laps. It was certainly not what I or any of us had imagined, and it was nothing that any of us had experienced in our lifetimes. As pastors became "televangelists," many having to figure out streaming

---

[14] Covenant Conversations is available at https://disciples.org/our-identity/covenant-conversation/.

for the first time, we stayed home from everything, including church. Going to the grocery store became a forage into the wild, and many of us washed our food containers down before putting them away, afraid and not knowing whether any of it might carry the deadly virus into our homes.

As more and more death surrounded us, we were not able to be present with those who were sick; and when death came, we were not able to gather to share in the grief and provide comfort and support. We used Zoom and FaceTime and other online tools to share in worship and carry out the business we needed to conduct. We prayed together online across our congregations and regions and held events for the whole denomination. We prepared digital elements for worship that Easter, which followed soon after the lockdown began. A sermon from me, music, and a communion service could simply be played for the online community, providing needed respite for pastors who were already exhausted from the constant crisis mode we found ourselves in each day.

Congregations who had been resistant to online giving platforms realized they needed to figure it out. Webinars about the various platforms were well-attended. The general ministries of the church met weekly to share information about how each was reimagining its work and using its resources to support congregations in their ministries and to support our clergy. Regional ministers met together online every week, checking in with one another and providing space for both lament and encouragement. Everywhere you turned, there was a story of doing something that had never been done before. The times required that we *had* to do things differently, for nothing about the world was the same as it had been.

There was no time to do a strategic plan to respond to COVID-19. More than ever, the church had to be focused on the service we were called to give, the love we were called to show. We couldn't use our buildings, and while we had always said that the congregation was never the building, we were living in that world now. We had to look at what we could do apart from those structures. "The buildings are closed, but the church has never closed," I said.

We learned how to work remotely, making investments in technology so that our ministry employees could continue the work. Meetings that had traditionally been held in person were now online, and they were productive. Never before had we or could we have imagined such a world, and yet here we were, making it all work with the help of God. The ministry; the fellowship of God's people; how to worship, study, and pray together were our focus. Congregations worked to ensure that they could continue their ministry to their local communities, and our general ministries provided resources and support to help make that happen where necessary.

We were living in a world in which the character of God and the example of Jesus Christ had to be at the heart of what we were doing. We understood perhaps as never before that this was our call, that this was truly our focus. We had no time or ability to say "not now." If we were to do ministry, we *had* to learn new things, we *had* to figure out a new way to do nearly everything. Creating connection and community and offering meaningful worship was clearly our priority, and we worked together to ensure that important ministries to our communities that were needed now more than ever could continue to flourish. Every life, every family, every congregation was precious, and our mission was to support their flourishing, no matter the context or demographic.

I found myself saying to others that I wished we could work together like this all the time, for in that crisis, our polity did not keep us from collaboration. We were prioritizing the vitality of our ministry, the ability for our congregations not only to worship but to continue serving their communities. We were able to put the sense of independence and autonomy that our denomination values in proper perspective, and my prayer was that somehow we would remember these lessons when things got better.

We lost so many lives, and our clergyfolk carried a heavy load trying to be a pastoral presence in the midst of so much sickness and grief. It took a toll that we couldn't have predicted. Yet we instinctively knew that we had to draw nearer to God in prayer and the Word. Regions went online not only to pray but to share ideas. We put a call out for people in the denomination who had technical skills to provide an online community in which to ask questions about everything from stronger Wi-Fi to cameras, sound, and streaming software. We wanted more than anything to stay in touch, to be in touch with our congregations, to feel that we were still a church, still a family … to know that we were not alone.

I began recording weekly videos to post online and started a weekly Facebook Live prayer time that I still lead consistently. We would never have imagined this world, but we leaned into God's spiritual power and love, and we were fed with the limitless creativity spurred by the Holy Spirit. We learned that we could build relationships online, even as we realized that there are times when there is no substitute for being with others, seeing them and experiencing that fellowship. But we knew that God heard us even though we weren't in the building. God was with us, and we were making our way to stay connected to each other. We were not alone. We could do new things, and we could do ministry in new ways.

Through those years of the pandemic, church leadership on the Governance Committee kept imagining how we could build a world that allowed more of our people to be engaged not only in fellowship, but in worship, study, and the decision making of the church that is so unique to our denomination. Regions and general ministries kept reimagining programs and rethinking how best to use resources for effective ministry, both within the congregation and region and in the wider community.

For the first time in history, we canceled the denomination's biennial session of the General Assembly, its highest decision-making body, scheduled for 2021. Our rules did not allow for that body to make decisions virtually. The rules were now glaringly out of step from how we needed to do our work. The Governance Committee continued to meet online, and we used the time to think hard and well not only about how our church might make its decisions, but about how we could create stronger connections between congregations, our middle judicatory, and our wider church. That sense of belonging to a wider whole can be elusive in a culture that rigorously values congregational autonomy; and in our conversations with people around the church, it became clear that far too many of us were, indeed, disconnected from how we functioned as a denomination. For those of us leading this work, the goal of creating more connection between our congregations and our wider church became the driving goal.

The proposed changes to *The Design* that were approved at the General Assembly meeting in Louisville in July 2023 came from nearly four years of prayer, engaging scripture, discernment, discussion, retreat, and conversations with theologians, historians, and past generations of leaders. Several of the changes had been brought before the church before but had not been approved. The pandemic certainly opened minds and hearts to understand that we not only *had* to do things differently, but that we *could* do things differently.

A smaller General Board, curated from across the life of the church, was part of the change. No longer limited to representatives sent from regions and general ministries, the General Board now seeks those with a wider variety of skills who can lend experience, expertise, imagination, and inspiration from a wider set of perspectives. With General Assembly moving from a biennial to a triennial cycle, online meetings of the Assembly will allow us to remove financial barriers to attendance at the in-person meetings. These digital sessions will provide much needed time for deeper conversations, learning, and discernment. We are no longer limited to twelve to twenty-four minutes of discussion on the floor as the only engagement about any issue or resolution. Those who have historically not been able to attend a meeting of the General Assembly because of cost will now be able to share online in a variety of modes: local gatherings that are connected to the wider online meeting or using a personal device can log in. We remain committed to having the voices from every congregation participating as part of the General Assembly.

These new rules create the opportunity for so many more Disciples from local congregations to engage, learn, and share their thoughts. We are the only mainline denomination that is so focused on allowing every congregation to have a voice at the highest levels of decision-making in the church. The pandemic made us all more comfortable with gathering online for various meetings and even worship. That experience made it easier for us to imagine how we might change how we gather as General Assembly.

As I write, an implementation team is preparing new rules to govern the meetings of the General Assembly. We are certainly moving into unknown territory, and we cannot be sure that everything will work exactly as we've imagined. But we do hold on to the power of our imaginations and to our courage to change. We have the ability to continue to make changes, to adjust here and there, to even take a different direction if at some point we determine this road is not the one we should be on. We have been given the authority by our governing documents—laid out by our forebears, who themselves understood that a time would come that they could not foresee. They knew that there was always going to be more work to do, and they gave us the freedom to change and prayed that we might have the courage and imagination to do so.

The road to the creation of *The Design* and our current denominational structure in 1969 was also filled with challenges. Not everything our forebears had hoped would happen came to fruition. Some proposed changes were rejected by various groups throughout the denomination. To be sure, *The Design* as a document is a grand compromise. There was, however, the hope that the church would continue to be self-reflective, to move forward and continue to be relevant. Our forebears who wrote *The Design* spoke of "continued renewal and structural reform" and hoped that we—their descendants and successors—would always be imagining, always be dreaming, always be praying about how our church could continue to be relevant to the world in which we live, how we could continue to be faithful to the gospel, and how we could continue to foster unity across the whole body of Christ.

Perhaps as never before, the COVID-19 pandemic created the urgency that necessitated a new way forward. It is indeed a new way forward, and the new processes will represent a shift in our culture regarding how we gather and make decisions. Moving forward will require that we have enough imagination to boldly consider that things might be different, that we can actually let go of some things and move in the direction to be a church that is always becoming. But the real hope is that we can become an ever more connected body, allowing our congregations to share in the visioning of who they are called to be, with regional and general ministries not only accompanying them but bringing new ideas for vital ministry to the table.

As we move forward to continue to evolve as a new church in a new world, we need to remind ourselves that everything begins with what we believe about God. I began this book with reflections on this important foundation. During one of my rereads of *The Prophetic Imagination,* I was struck by words in Brueggemann's preface to the book's fortieth anniversary edition.

> [T]here are two types of imagination, that of "the generals and their opponents," or that of consumer theology and its resisters. The fact is that we in American [and Canadian] society too easily live "inside this imagination when prophetic imagination is capable of enabling us to live "inside God's imagination."
>
> What the prophet tradition knows is that it could be different, and the difference can be enacted. ... The capacity of such alternative imagination is neither strong nor wise. But clearly,
>
> ***God's foolishness is wiser than human wisdom, and God's weakness is stronger than human strength.*** *Consider your own call, brothers and sisters: not many of you were wise by human standards, not many were powerful, not many were of noble birth. But God chose what is foolish in the world to shame the wise; God chose what is weak in the world to shame the strong; God chose what is low and despised in the world, things that are not, to abolish things that are* (1 Corinthians 1:25–28; emphasis added).[15]

The call is not just to dream, but to listen, discern, decide, and act to bring the alternate reality to fruition. To imagine that the world actually can be different than what we see because of Jesus Christ

---

[15] Walter Brueggemann, *The Prophetic Imagination: 40th Anniversary Edition* (Minneapolis: Fortress Press, 2018), 30.

requires that we are willing to work together to bring about justice, mercy, and kindness in our world. This all flows from an understanding of God's limitless love. If I love my neighbor, I want for him or her what I want for myself—a world in which each person can flourish and everyone has enough.

Let us pause for a minute and go back to what we believe about God. If we have established the overwhelming authority, power, and goodness of God—if we truly believe those "omni" words—living inside God's imagination means that we do not limit our vision of what can be done, for we are leaning and depending on an all-powerful, all-knowing, all-loving, limitless God. To even dream such is, as Brueggemann notes, "neither strong nor wise." But because we seek God's "foolishness" and not just human wisdom, what we imagine *is* possible. It can be done. I daresay that if you do not believe in the limitless nature of God, then we should abandon a charade of being church, of being followers of Jesus.

Think of examples in your own congregation or community when someone dared to imagine that ministry could be done differently. We are all too quick to impose limits that are derived from human norms, norms that are generally established to ensure power for certain people and the institutions created to protect it. Our human "wisdom" cannot be the arbiter of what God desires or what is possible with and through God. Whenever we resist change, we are actually resisting a threat to a comfort level that provides us with either comfort or power … sometimes both.

The modern, Western church is an institution, created over time to resemble secular institutions and imbued with the understanding of power that is so intrinsic to many human institutions. It is my experience, not only in the church but in other institutional settings in which I have given leadership, that those who are the most uncomfortable with proposed change are those who benefit the most from the status quo. Even when the breaking down of barriers allows new voices to enter the space, the danger is that those new voices will settle down in a system that preserves power as they have come to understand it. The more familiar folks are with the system, the more power they can accrue and the less interested they are in making any change that will alter their power position.

It is also true that when imagination casts vision for change that empowers those who do not currently benefit from the existing system, it is those people who then see themselves in the change and are inspired and encouraged by it. We must always be on guard not to merely assume the power positions of any system and to become comfortable as the system begins to confer power on us. Around the world we see in history those nations who, having resisted colonial power, now take up the same authoritative tools of the very empire that oppressed them, building their own power base that looks remarkably the same as that of their oppressors. Given the racist structures that continue to permeate the United States, a predominantly White denomination such as mine must also be wary of allowing those subconscious norms to limit its ability to bring about the kindom of God where all are welcome.

Our church has for decades named being an anti-racist church as a priority. We have worked to create training to help clergy and congregations be aware of their biases of all kinds, trying to ensure that the processes of the church are themselves anti-racist. And yet there are those who resist this direction, and we have a long way to go before all of us fully embrace this vision. To do so challenges the very roots of the institution, born as it was on the "frontier" in the early nineteenth century, grounded in an understanding of American individualism and independence and in a time when church movements were split on their views about slavery.

Churches are human institutions. Over time, we have come to care more for the institutions we have created than for the gospel message they were supposed to help us share. If we allow ourselves, we can become so mired in egalitarian processes that we are blind to God's imagination. We can be so focused on our insistence on doctrinal positions that we allow those differences to water down our ability to coalesce for the building of the kindom. We can become more concerned about exacting orthodox adherence to dogma or doctrine than we are about what we are doing to demonstrate our love of neighbor.

Imagine what we might do together if we allowed that we are not the single arbiters of God's truth, that we are called rather to love and embrace human dignity and to seek the flourishing and well-being of all God's creation. What if we didn't argue about certain Bible passages, but instead worked together to ensure that our communities enjoyed safe, affordable housing, health care for all, and schools whose quality is not contingent upon property values? What if the lens we use to read the Bible is the lens of God's limitless love? What if we were not so concerned about who presides at the Lord's table and instead were more concerned that everyone feels welcome at that table? We can no longer say with certainty what we cannot do, for the COVID-19 pandemic showed us in many ways that we can, in fact, do things we never imagined.

The mythical *Sankofa* bird—with its feet facing forward and its head reaching back to grab an egg in its beak—is a representation of the Ghanaian philosophy that it is important to reach back and take what we need from the past to move forward into the future. We need not and cannot discard all that has brought us to this point in time. In fact, we will need that history and DNA of our various traditions to live authentically into the future.

But if we are to live inside God's imagination, we must be true to God's call to love without limits. If we believe that God is able to do far beyond all that we can ask or think, we must understand that the world will often not see what we do as wise or opportune. There is quite honestly nothing about the good news of Jesus Christ that is rational, at least not to the human mind. We require the power of God's Holy Spirit to be able to love as Jesus loved. Our testimony rests on the fact that, without God, without the power of the Holy Spirit, we cannot do what we are called to do.

As we trust in this limitless God, we gain the freedom to imagine beyond what we see, believing that God is able to accomplish it. In yielding our imperfect selves the One whose kin[g]dom knows no end, we open up the very windows of heaven, helping to make real God's kin[g]dom here on earth.

REFLECTION

1. Think of a time when you and/or others were able to imagine an alternate way of doing things in church. What inspired you? How was the idea received?

2. What experiences did you have during the COVID-19 pandemic that opened your imagination to how different things could be?

3. What is the importance of getting "inside God's imagination"? How does this open your mind to new possibilities?

4. If you could imagine an alternate society to the one in which we live, what would it be like? What steps would you take to begin implementing that vision?

Let's Be the Church We Say We Are

Your church or denomination likely has one or more of these statements intended to signal its focus and guide its ministry: vision statement, mission statement, identity statement, strategic plan, mission priorities, or something like that. It is certainly important for any ministry to name its vision and mission and to lay out its priorities. Vision statements are used to set a long-term goal for the future, what you hope your organization will be or achieve in the future. Mission statements define what you are doing now to achieve that future state. Identity statements help you clarify who you are and who you want to be.

I've participated in task forces charged with developing these statements, and it is often a time-consuming process. You try to craft a statement that says enough to be definitive but without so much detail that it limits how you proceed. New leaders often seize on these statements to make their initial mark. New language can give people a sense of moving forward, taking a different direction, of making a difference. For many events, we choose themes and we produce all kinds of paraphernalia, "swag," to reinforce those themes, and even the statements. We talk about "branding" our ministries, and we want logos that will translate well to T-shirts, caps, and bags. And we hope that all these strategies will get the words we've crafted into people's minds and hearts.

Yes, I have participated in these creative endeavors. I love the power of language and how words can inspire and energize. And yet I fear that sometimes we are too caught up in the lingo, the branding, and the hype. We are often content to use our words to promote ideas, but we quite often do not focus on how we can live into the words.

Allow me to use my own tradition as an example of how to examine our language and ask how we are living into it.

My church has a wonderful identity statement: "We are Disciples of Christ, a movement for wholeness in a fragmented world. As part of the one Body of Christ, we welcome all to the Lord's Table as God has welcomed us." This is a well-known statement, embraced by most congregations. When I first began serving as the head of the denomination, my thought was this: We have wonderful words, wonderful statements. We don't need new language to describe who we are. *We just need to be the church we say we are.* If we are a movement for wholeness, how do we embody that? If we say we welcome all to the Lord's table, we should have no issues with churches rejecting persons with particular identities to the table or the congregation, and yet this kind of exclusion and injustice abounds. It begs the question: Do we truly want to be who we say we are? If so, why are there still churches that exclude persons with particular identities from the Lord's table and their community altogether?

Going back to the building blocks of this book, if we believe God is all-knowing, all-loving, why aren't we loving? If we love our neighbor, don't we want the same things for our neighbor that we want for ourselves? Do our ministry priorities reflect that understanding? Are we working for affordable housing, living wages, clean water, and quality education that is not dependent upon a zip code? One of our priorities is to become an anti-racist church. And yet we have clergy and congregations who avoid the topic altogether.

Our polity does not demand anything in terms of compliance, but if you are a part of us and you say you believe these things, why are you not committed to doing them? Love grounds our understanding of inclusion, for, as I have repeated often in this text, we cannot limit God's love. We are not the arbiters of who is included. If we can limit God, then God is not God, and Jesus cannot be who we claim he is.

In order to be true to what we say we believe, the world has to see the coherence between our words and our actions. It is the inconsistency between who we say we are and how we act that is the greatest detriment to the reception of the good news of Jesus Christ. If the goal is to stay at the table, we must share a common commitment to spiritual practice as the grounding for our lives in community. We cannot stay at the table despite differences and we cannot be who we say we are unless we are committed to the practice of the way of Jesus. As Christians, no matter your affiliation or tradition, I pray we might find common ground here.

Spiritual Practices

How do we move from embracing words and ideas to truly living into active ministry? One of the biggest failures in mainline Christianity today is that far too many of us are spiritually dry; we fail to emphasize biblical literacy and spiritual practices or ground our discipleship in these practices. By literacy, I do not meet dogmatic interpretations that are considered "correct." Biblical literacy is a lifestyle of continuous, faithful reading and critical study of the biblical text. Yes, the text can be difficult; that's why we must develop the skills to wrestle with it.

Learning what is in the text is the first step, and we should make this an integral part of spiritual formation for all those in our congregations, across all age groups. Practices that deepen and grow our spirituality—practices such as prayer, meditation, worship, and journaling—are important to help us engage the presence of the Holy and invite us to read scripture with the help of the Holy Spirit. Developing habits that allow us to become familiar with what that presence feels like, how it manifests for each person, is important. When our congregations focus on developing these spiritual practices, they are grounded in an understanding that their focus is to build a community that reflects the difference Jesus can make. We must believe that we are "called to be the presence of Christ in our community," that they are called to bear witness to and reflect the limitless love of God in all they do.

As a child, my now thirty-something son always began his bedtime prayer with the words, "God, I wish that you would ..." We never tried to give him different language because we wanted him to be comfortable in his own approach to prayer. In Sunday school, he learned the stories from the Bible that give us the narrative of how

God has acted in human history and the Christian narrative of Jesus' birth, life, death, and resurrection.

My young niece often asked questions during her bedtime prayer time, and her mother would text me with those questions. Because I was a minister, my niece believed that I could answer all of her questions about God, or at least give her something to think about. It gave her mother and me the opportunity to let her know that some questions are beyond us, but that God is real, God loves you, and it is okay to ask questions of and about God.

On the drive to school, my husband had our son read a daily passage from Proverbs using *The One Year Bible*.[16] One summer, he actually wrote a journal about the lessons he had learned from his school-ride reading of Proverbs. It was amazing to see how an elementary school child could share what the scriptural text meant to him. He was using a modern translation that was easier to understand than, say, the *King James Version*. He was expressing his thoughts in his own words, putting the truths he had gleaned down on paper in ways that made sense to him. It let us know that the practice had taken root. To this day, one of his favorite mantras is simply, "Lean not!" Proverbs 3:5 has stayed with him into adulthood, and those two words capture his approach to trusting God.

Now we have established a habit with our two-year-old grandson for mealtime grace. It is wonderful to see him clasp his hands before eating, looking to us to say, "It's time to say grace." Even when asking for a second helping, he will clasp his hands again before eating.

The most important aspect of establishing such habits with our children and grandchildren is that we model these behaviors. When we demonstrate that prayer or reading the Bible is simply a part of our lives because of our faith, we can also help them to be comfortable with asking questions and build a capacity for critical thinking about faith, just as we work to build critical thinking skills in other subjects. Small, habitual routines aid in the spiritual formation of our children. Once they are of an appropriate age, their decision about confessing

---

[16] *The One Year Bible NLT* (Carol Stream, IL: Tyndale House Publishers, 1996).

Christ is their own, but creating open and safe spaces both for spiritual practice and questions is an important part of our children's formation, and it begins to develop their capacity for discernment in their own faith journey.

Congregations and pastors who value these spiritual practices then move into mission with an understanding of their ministry as the impetus instead of pursuing service projects as a form of charity that many other nonprofit organizations might do. One can do "good works" as part of any number of nonprofit service organizations. But Christians do so because of the teachings of Jesus, which call for us to feed the hungry, visit the sick, and attend to those in prison, as Jesus taught in Matthew 25. The prophets repeatedly proclaimed God's command to care for the widow, the orphan, and the stranger. Micah 6:8 calls us to "do justice, love kindness and walk humbly with your God." Grounding ourselves in the teachings of Jesus and the commandments of God helps us to realize that our actions should be consistent with the teachings of Christ. Our "why" is to lift up the good news of Jesus and bear witness to God's limitless love. In so doing, we pray that the work we do helps others to seek the love of God alongside us.

In my tradition, we believe the Holy Spirit is available to each of us to open up the truth of God's word. Because we are committed to a diversity of perspectives—be they theological, ideological, or political—we do not insist on agreement on a particular biblical interpretation. However, in order to wrestle, in order to engage with one another as we seek deeper understanding, we do have to know what is actually written in the text. As a divinity school student, I was amazed that a few of my fellow students were not as familiar with the biblical text as I was. Granted, I was a second-career student, some fifteen years or so older than many in my cohort. However, I grew up in a church where we learned Bible verses, learned the books of the Bible and the order they appeared. As I grew older, I was blessed to have Sunday school and Baptist Training Union (BTU) teachers who invited us to ask questions, to discuss topics that were relevant to our teen experiences. I became a member of the Disciples of Christ as a young adult, and my home church instilled a love of the text, but also a responsibility to engage the text critically, to be a student of the text alongside the teachers and leaders. Those who have teaching and preaching gifts help us to learn and engage the text. The Holy Spirit is there to help each one of us come to an understanding of what the text has said and what it means to us in our time.

Historically, the Bible has sometimes been used to justify oppression, hatred, and exclusion. From slavery to the rejection of women and the LGBTQ+ community, the words of scripture have been used to exclude and demean people. In current political circles, there are those who are trying to use the stories of ancient kings to legitimize leaders who themselves do not operate in alignment with Christian principles of love and respect for human dignity.

If we believe that God is love—if we believe that God's love is limitless, barring no one—the only lens we can use in scripture is that of God's love. For Christians, that love is revealed in the person of Jesus Christ. Any interpretation that would deny this love is inconsistent with this God. Any attempt to justify oppression, hatred, and disregard for human life cannot be condoned by convoluted interpretations of scripture. I have heard it said that if the interpretation does not reflect God's love for all, then the interpretation is wrong. I agree with this position simply because, as I have now said repeatedly, I stand firmly on my belief in the bigness of God, the deep and limitless love of God, and that God's welcome at the table is available to all.

There are many approaches to studying the Bible. Churches must continue to invest in curricula that speak to all ages and generations. Modes of instruction should keep pace with advances in technology and should be considered in light of the issues of the current context. People want to know what God has to say that is relevant to their lives today. Because we know that none of us has the only right answer, we have to develop the capacity to engage scripture critically, placing it in proper historical contexts, understanding linguistic complications that arise as a result of translation, including problems in translating idiomatic phrases.

The best gift we can give our church is this capacity to engage. Questions are simply part of the process of engagement and seeking to understand. From the innocent questions of curious children to the angst-ridden explorations of adults who have endured trauma and hurt, Christians must pass on a tradition of knowing the text that is coupled with an appreciation for critical engagement. Too many have been hurt by pedantic interpretations and the shutting down of those who are merely seeking greater clarity on the questions that invade their lives.

Health psychology researcher Philippa Lally published a study in the *European Journal of Social Psychology*[17] that explored how long it actually takes to establish a habit. The results indicated that it takes at least two months—or sixty-six days, to be exact. Depending on the behavior, it may take up to two hundred and fifty-four days! Spiritual practices of prayer and Bible study can begin with just a few minutes a day. When I teach Sunday school or a Bible study, I always challenge my students to begin with just five minutes a day. You can use a devotional or Bible reading plan to help guide your personal devotional time. Perhaps you begin with a brief prayer and then read a few verses of scripture or the entry from a devotional. For your children, the first spiritual practice might be a blessing for meals or a bedtime prayer. Consistency in these practices helps to establish the importance of speaking to God, whether to give thanks or to pray for family and friends.

When we study the Bible, we often have to overcome cynicism formed by experiences people have had as children or adults. Countless people have been hurt and have turned away from the church because of interpretations that diminished their identity and humanity. There are Christians who want to use the words of scripture to support their own understandings of societal norms. Too often, we do not equip people in the pews with tools to faithfully and critically engage scripture and discern an understanding. It is important to know both what the text

---

[17] P. Lally et al., "How Are Habits Formed: Modelling Habit Formation in the Real World," *European Journal of Social Psychology* 40, no. 6, October 2010, 998–1009.

meant in its ancient or original context, but also how it might speak to us in our contemporary context. As I've said before, the lens of the love of God is always the most appropriate and faithful window to understanding God's word.

Years ago, I developed a Bible study for the congregation I pastored using Disciples founder Alexander Campbell's *Principles of Interpretation*. Published in *The Millenial Harbinger*, Campbell's journal, in which he shared his ideas for Christian reform and the role of the church in bringing about the "millenium," a time when the kingdom of God would be made evident on Earth.[18]

When I pastored in Downers Grove, Illinois, I had begun a weekly Bible study, and I wanted to find something that would connect congregants to the Disciples' perspective on studying the Bible. One of the elders who was the child of a Disciples minister said that she grew up with the understanding that not only was it possible for her to discern the truth of God's word but it was her *responsibility* as a Christian.

There are many perspectives and templates for "how to study the Bible." I offer my reflections on Campbell's *Principles of Interpretation*[19] because I think they offer a way to consider how we invite the text to speak to us in our current context. Campbell expressed the hope that if everyone was applying the same principles for interpreting the Bible, there might be a greater chance of unity within the body of Christ. Even though he offered these principles, I'd like to believe he understood that such unanimity is likely not possible, given the nature of human discourse. Even with knowledge of historical context, linguistic acumen, and biblical scholarship, we must concede that we have limited ways of getting inside the heads of the writers of the various books of the Bible. Each of us will come to the text with the formation of our childhood faith traditions, the

---

[18] You can learn more about *The Millenial Harbinger* at https://discipleshistory.org/wiki/millennial-harbinger-the/.

[19] *The Millennial Harbinger*, https://webfiles.acu.edu/departments/Library/HR/restmov_nov11/www.mun.ca/rels/restmov/texts/acampbell/mh1846/TFTP03.HTM. The Millenial Harbinger is also available online via the Disciples of Christ Historical Society.

cynicism that life offers, and the diversity of our own experiences, personal beliefs, and theological formation. In a world rife with divisions based on biblical interpretations, Campbell's conclusions are hopeful as a perspective across all Christian traditions. Campbell believed that we cannot lay claim to concrete certainty, but he offers that perhaps the most faithful thing we can do as we engage scripture is to get "within the understanding distance." I hope you'll find a place for yourself there.

Here are the seven rules Campbell listed in *Principles of Interpretation*, followed by my own reflection on them. I acknowledge that I am not a biblical scholar, but I have found Campbell's framework to be insightful.

> Rule 1. On opening any book in the sacred scriptures, consider first the historical circumstances of the book. These are the order, the title, the author, the date, the place, and the occasion of it.
>
> Rule 2. In examining the contents of any book, as respects precepts, promises, exhortations, &c. observe who it is that speaks, and under what dispensation he officiates. Is he a Patriarch, a Jew, or a Christian? Consider also the persons addressed—their prejudices, characters, and religious relations. Are they Jews or Christians—believers or unbelievers—approved or disapproved? This rule is essential to the proper application of every command, promise, threatening, admonition, or exhortation, in Old Testament or New.

For many of us who studied in seminary, until recent decades the historical-critical method of biblical interpretation was standard teaching. Even though this method has fallen somewhat out of favor, it is important as we read any book of the Bible to explore who wrote it, when, where, and why it was written. Many scholars will also insist that you must understand the genre of each book, for example, history, poetry, gospel, or epistle. When we know who wrote the book, the historical times in which that person lived, and the circumstances and purposes that led to the writing of the text, we have that important context.

For example, it's important to know that Moses actually did not physically write the first books of the Old Testament. But we can engage how they came to be and why. What purposes were served by their creation, and how do they speak to us today? Who were the audiences for each text? Was the writer speaking to his own people of the same culture or the same faith? Was it written for believers or nonbelievers?

As you read the words of each book, think about who is speaking and to whom. What was the purpose of the dialogue, and what cultural cues from that historical period must we understand to better interpret what we are reading? All of these considerations can alter how we understand what the text meant in its original context. If we have a clearer idea of its original intent and meaning, we can more effectively consider what it means for us today and how or whether it speaks to us in our context.

There are excellent study Bibles that provide both historical and archaeological information alongside the text. To understand the scriptures, you must know the history of ancient Israel, its history of kings and prophets, its experiences as a people in diaspora, the role of the prophets in keeping the people's hope in God alive, and what those people thought the Messiah would mean to them. If you know that Nazareth was considered a "backwater town," and if you understand that engaged women who became pregnant were considered adulterous and thus subject to death by stoning, you can understand Joseph's story in Matthew and people's reluctance to accept Jesus as the chosen one. Context opens up the text and gives us a way to discern its contemporary relevance for us.

If we consider our relationships at the table, it is important to understand their history, experience, cultural context, and traditions in order to honestly engage them. Human lives are texts in many ways. When we make assumptions or come to relationships with a lack of honest curiosity or lack a desire to see people as they truly are, the meaning of their lives and opinions will escape us, and we will be the poorer because of our own arrogance.

> Rule 3. To understand the meaning of what is commanded, promised, taught, &c., the same philological principles, deduced from the nature of language, or the same laws of interpretation which are applied to the language of other books, are to be applied to the language of the Bible.
>
> Rule 4. Common usage, which can only be ascertained by testimony, must always decide the meaning of any word which has but one signification; but when words have according to testimony (i.e., the Dictionary) more meanings than one, whether literal or figurative, the scope, the context, or parallel passages must decide the meaning; for if common usage, the design of the writer, the context, and parallel passages fail, there can be no certainty in the interpretation of language.
>
> Rule 5. In all tropical language ascertain the point of resemblance, and judge of the nature of the trope, and its kind, from the point of resemblance.
>
> Rule 6. In the interpretation of symbols, types, allegories, and parables, this rule is supreme. Ascertain the point to be illustrated; for comparison is never to be extended beyond that point—to all the attributes, qualities, or circumstances of the symbol, type, allegory, or parable.

Rules 3–6 address the importance of understanding the language of the Bible. Not just the language of translation, but an understanding of the original languages in which the Old and New Testaments were written: Hebrew and Koine Greek. If you have studied another language besides your native language, you are aware that there is often not a word-for-word exchange between two languages. Over time, languages also change; new vocabulary arrives on the scene, and some words pass from popular usage.

For example, in the scriptural text, idioms have different understandings and uses in every language, and the work of translation and exegesis requires that you do that kind of parsing. If you don't possess those language skills, there are resources that can help you in digging into what the original text actually meant. The work of a faithful pastor or Bible teacher is getting inside the original language as a way of opening up the interpretation. Languages in the ancient world may have used tropes and idioms that are not familiar or applicable to us in the present day. The important point here is that spending some time exploring the original language can greatly help in the process of exploring what God is saying to us through the Bible. It's good to remember as well, as biblical scholar Amy Jill Levine has noted, that we cannot be so constructionist as to imply that all that God has to say was said in the ancient text. It leaves no work for the Holy Spirit to do with us as we read the text in our time. Surely, God is still speaking.[20]

> Rule 7. For the salutary and sanctifying intelligence of the oracles of God, the following rule is indispensable: *We must come within the understanding distance.* (emphasis added)

Perhaps Alexander Campbell's most important contribution to biblical interpretation is this: "We must come within the understanding distance." Given that we are discerning what God is saying—what God has said through the instruments of human minds and pens over centuries, all of the rules and strategies to determine what is being said in the biblical texts—we are limited in so many ways. The writers of those texts were limited just as we are to their own languages. Human language is limited when we are trying to describe the work of the Creator God in history.

The gospels are not chronological histories; they were constructed to make a case about who Jesus is. They have authority when we understand their purpose and content. I believe that scripture is inspired by God but it was written by humans (actually, by men), who themselves had particular backgrounds, contexts, purposes, and perspectives. The biblical text is complicated and in some places difficult to understand, let alone discern meaning.

---

[20] Amy Jill Levine, "Amy Jill Levine: How to Read the Bible's 'Clobber Passages' on Homosexuality," Outreach, September 9, 2022, https://www.chicagomanualofstyle.org/tools_citationguide/citation-guide-1.html#cg-news.

After we have worked through a good translation, done our important historical contextual analysis, exegesis, and so on, we are left with the reality that the closest we can get is that "understanding distance." Taking texts out of their context is never helpful, and being literal usually ignores the reality that we do not live in the time or among the people in which the text is situated. The more we study scripture, however, I believe the great commandment is an important lens for interpretation. If the interpretation we have goes against the command to love God and love our neighbor, if it places any limitations on that love of God or on God's ability to do more than we can humanly imagine, that interpretation cannot be consistent with the God of love and the incarnate Christ we follow. Scripture cannot be used to demonize or diminish the humanity of another or build any kind of obstruction to being in the community of God.

Most importantly, as Christians the Bible is our sacred text and it holds authority for our faith. A lifelong habit of exploration of that text—of considering the works of scholars, preachers, and our fellow Christians on the journey—must be a part of our engagement with the text.

I love my own time of daily scripture reading, but I think our engagement together in community is necessary and perhaps even more valuable. There are lay teachers whose gifts have guided many a person not only to a deeper understanding but to a more vibrant lifestyle of engagement with the sacred text. My own seminary journey was greatly enhanced because of all my years of Bible study in groups at my church.

Before accepting a call to vocational ministry, leading others in wrestling with the Bible was a core part of my lay ministry. Such knowledge of the text later enabled me to better understand the various academic frameworks that were taught to me. Although I was unfamiliar with the academic theories, I did have a deep familiarity with the text itself, and that served me well. You need not have a seminary degree to engage scripture faithfully. Someone once asked me what I would require of the church if I could do so. My answer was, "Bible study in every congregation." Not dogma or orthodoxy, but engagement and exploration. I invite us all to remain humble in that practice and to seek faithfully to at least be within the "understanding distance."

Contemplative Practices

I often say that, just as diet and exercise are the keys to physical health, Bible study and prayer are the building blocks for spiritual health. Depending on your background, you may have a particular experience of prayer. I grew up being asked to give a "sentence prayer" at the close of Sunday school. It was not something I was given time to write out, but something I was asked to speak from my heart, on the spot.

If you grew up in church, you are probably used to a certain "church-ese"—words and phrases we hear often in prayers in church. If your tradition uses written prayers and more formal liturgies, you are likely used to certain phrases. If your tradition sees prayer as a form of worship that comes straight from your heart in the moment, you are also probably used to a certain vocabulary. You may remember a pastor, elder, or deacon who used a particular phrase in his or her prayers all the time, and you remember it clearly. I know many people who would never dream of praying in a public setting without writing it down, and I know others who don't understand why you would need to write down a prayer. Our corporate prayer life in church includes prayers of welcoming God's presence (invocation), intercession (prayers of the people, sharing joys and concerns), and supplication (often an altar call or pastoral prayer). All prayers should include some initial words of thanksgiving to God. But what is your private prayer life like? If the only time you pray is when someone else is praying while you are gathered with others in worship, I am concerned about your spiritual health.

The best model for spiritual practice we have is Jesus himself. He frequently went off by himself to pray alone. Every time he was challenged or given "test" questions from the priests, scribes, and Pharisees, his response invariably came from scripture. He didn't use scripture to condemn but, rather, to clarify, teach, and admonish when necessary. We often think of the Lord's Prayer, which was given when the disciples asked Jesus to teach them to pray, or the prayer Jesus prayed in Gethsemane the night before the crucifixion as the most important examples of Jesus praying. But in John 17, Jesus prays for us. Jesus prays for all those who will come to believe in him because of the witness of those he has taught. He prays that they/we would have the same relationship with God that he has. That relationship is one of frequent and intimate engagement with God in prayer. Jesus' time alone in prayer with God was his time to find strength and peace for the work he was called to do. He went alone to pray; he focused on time alone with God.

For many years, my daily devotional practice has included a centering prayer. To aid me in this practice, I use an app from Contemplative Outreach (available at https://contemplativeoutreach.org), which describes centering prayer as a method of prayer that is "both a relationship with God and a discipline to deepen that relationship." You begin with choosing a sacred word that you will use to focus your time of silence. The goal is to rid your mind of outside thoughts and to be open to listening to what God and the Holy Spirit may be saying to you. Being still and quiet and keeping random thoughts out of our minds can be a challenge. Focusing on your sacred word helps to keep those thoughts at bay. It is recommended that you practice centering prayer for twenty minutes a day. While I was still a bivocational pastor with a very busy corporate position, I would often start my day by closing the door to my office and taking fifteen or twenty minutes for centering prayer. Over time, I got better at clearing my mind and truly being still before God.

The benefits of centering prayer are not only spiritual but physical. When you allow yourself to be still in that kind of disciplined way, you use deep breaths to help center you. Deep breathing helps to slow your heart rate and lower your blood pressure and can help to dissolve stress. That kind of stillness allows you to have the experience of entering into a sacred space that you intentionally create in order to be open to what it feels like to be in the presence of God. Each of us has a different sacred word, a different ritual or protocol to take us in and out of our centering time. The app I use gives me the ability to use a particular tone to sound the beginning and end of my time. I now have a singing bowl that allows me to create my own live sound to begin my time of prayer. It is the silence that makes the difference, and it is the continued practice that moves us from mere ritual to meaning.

Father Richard Rohr of the Center for Action and Contemplation writes:

> When we emphasize specific practices too much, contemplation can become a matter of technique and performance. We fall back into self-analysis: Am I doing the practice correctly? The revelation of God, who always wants to enter the material world as our image, cannot possibly depend upon people sitting silently on a prayer cushion twice a day. That would mean that 99.9 percent of people who have ever lived on this earth have not known God. The definition of Christian contemplation up until recent times has come from the early monastic and desert traditions, but the field is far bigger than that.
>
> Parker Palmer writes, "The function of contemplation in all its forms is to penetrate illusion and help us to touch reality." I think he's right and I would add that great love and great suffering are the normal paths of transformation. There's an important place for practices of contemplation. I'm not throwing them out, but any practice of contemplation is for the sake of helping us sustain what we temporarily learn through great love or great suffering, whether it's on a honeymoon or the day after a parent dies. When we're in the middle of great grief or great love, we become a nondual thinker for a few days, weeks, or months, but we all know it doesn't last. It doesn't last—unless we put it into practice.[21]

The difference in my own spirit and well-being when I do *not* do centering prayer or some form of quiet meditation is obvious to me,

---

[21] Richard Rohr, "The Purpose of Contemplation," Center for Action and Contemplation, September 22, 2024, https://cac.org/daily-meditations/the-purpose-of-contemplation/.

and sometimes to others. My spiritual director once commented in a session that I seemed to be very peaceful. I can often have an intensity about everything I do, and when I'm engaged, my conversation is lively and energetic. When I really care about a topic, the intensity comes through in my voice. On this particular day, I had not done centering prayer until the end of my workday, before I went to meet with my spiritual director. I arrived in a very quiet mood, a place where I would normally begin the day. Because my spiritual director often saw me at the end of my day, it struck her that my spirit was in a different place. Since then, I try to take a few minutes before an evening meeting or during a conference to do centering prayer to ground and settle myself.

During 2024, I was introduced to a curriculum titled "Compassion Practice" in a class taught by Rev. Dale Suggs and his wife, Shelly Suggs, of the BE**LOVED** WAY Compassion Network. Dale is pastor of BE**LOVED**, a Disciples community in California.

Based on the work of Dr. Frank Rogers, who taught for years at Claremont School of Theology, "Compassion Practice" focuses on the discipline of spiritual practice to deepen our compassion for ourselves first and, ultimately, to increase our ability to show compassion to others, even those with whom we disagree, even those we simply don't like. It reinforces the concept that before you can help others, you have to help yourself. The three-level course begins with working on deepening your own contemplative practices.

From centering prayer to guided meditations, I found participating in this online course helped to re-light my fire around my own practices. One of my favorite exercises is a meditation that asks you to visualize your favorite place, a place where you have experienced God in some way. Using visualization, you are encouraged to remember that place through regular practice. There will be moments when you need to bring the presence of the Holy into the space with you, and being able to literally call on it can be a powerful tool to help you show compassion for yourself and for others and to help you to keep the misbehavior of others from negatively affecting you. The reality is that, unless we are able to be in authentic community with others, our own practices will not reflect the God with whom we desire to be in relationship. We do not follow Jesus alone; we do not do ministry alone. I endorse this program enthusiastically.

When we as Christians are not making investments in our spiritual health—when we are living as communities that have no theological or biblical grounding for who we are and why we do what we do—we become spiritually dry. We do not need the church for good coffee after worship. Many people have other options for social networks and even for doing various kinds of service for the community. But we as Christians are called to be in compassionate community with one another, loving each other as Christ loved us and reflecting the limitless love of God to the world. In our service as faithful people, the kindness we show, the justice for which we advocate is done because of our faith in Christ.

We know that people are seeking ways to make meaning in their lives. People want to make a difference in the world, and they gravitate toward groups and places that are contributing to the well-being of the community and the world. But we also know that making meaning requires more than just activities. It is because of our faithful disciplines that we prepare ourselves to wholeheartedly serve our communities, advocating for justice and human flourishing. Our congregations will not see vitality unless the spiritual work is done, which feeds the work we do as witnesses in the world.

I love fresh-cut flowers, and my husband loves to give me flowers. After several days, however, the leaves wither, the blooms shrivel. Have you ever touched a dried bouquet of flowers? The blooms will often crumble when you touch them. Dried leaves can sometimes be so brittle they can cut you. Psalm 1 teaches us the importance of this spiritual grounding, particularly in the Word of God:

> *Happy are those*
> *who do not follow the advice of the wicked*
> *or take the path that sinners tread*
> *or sit in the seat of scoffers,*
> *but their delight is in the law of the LORD,*

> *and on his law they meditate day and night.*
> *They are like trees*
>   *planted by streams of water,*
> *which yield their fruit in its season,*
>   *and their leaves do not wither.*
> *In all that they do, they prosper.* (Psalms 1:1–3)

Spiritual practices allow us to grow deep roots that will help us to withstand the storms of life. Trees that are planted by streams of water have roots that reach far down into the earth to get the nourishment they need. When we are not thus grounded, we cannot bear the fruit of love and service that our discipleship requires. Like the withered leaves of dried flowers, when we are dry, we can either crumble or, worse, we can "cut" others. Service and ministry without spiritual growth and maturity can actually damage the cause of Christ and harm the very ones we want to reach. "Church hurt" is often the result of experiences with people who belong to churches, say they are Christian, but—because they are spiritually dry—are hurtful, hateful, lack compassion, and diminish the human dignity of those they deem not to be worthy of inclusion.

People are seeking something meaningful and real that transforms them, something that gives them strength and hope. Deep relationship with God through prayer and the Word gives us courage, allows us to imagine as we embrace God's imagination. Deepening our relationship with God makes our ministry vital, relevant, and—most of all—loving. Deep relationship with God gives us the freedom to change, the freedom to continually ask ourselves how we can better reflect the love and glory of God as Jesus taught us. Just as faith without works is dead, prayer without action is empty. From that place of deep relationship, we can offer Jesus to other people as the source of our own transformation. Most importantly, with this engagement, we can participate with God to create the kindom God has imagined for us.

In today's religious, environmental, and political climate, our compassionate engagement is urgent and vital. When we experience the reality of our oneness with God, others, and

Creation, actions of justice and healing naturally follow. If we're working to create a more whole world, contemplation can give our actions nonviolent, loving power for the long haul.[22]

In addition to the Bible, it is important to feed our spirits and minds with the writings of those whose insights can inspire and challenge us. I have always been inspired by the prolific words of Dr. Martin Luther King Jr. If you have not read *Why We Can't Wait*[23] or anything besides the "I Have a Dream" speech, you will find that this pastor, theologian, and drum major for justice had a lot to say that is still relevant even more than five decades after his assassination.

Dr. King's major influences—Benjamin Mays and Howard Thurman—are also part of my regular reading. Thurman's *Jesus and the Disinherited*[24] is a classic that is worth your engagement. I have already mentioned my reading of Walter Brueggemann and my engagement with the devotional writing of Father Richard Rohr. I also enjoy newer collections such as *Psalms for Black Lives: Reflections for the Work of Liberation* by Gabby Cudjoe-Wilkes and Andrew Wilkes[25]; *anything* by Anne Lamott; *Black Liturgies: Prayers, Poems and Meditations for Staying Human*[26] by Cole Arthur Riler; and *The Lives We Actually Have: 100 Blessings for Imperfect Days*[27] by Kate Bowler and Jessica Richie. There are so many others in my rotation that are resources for my own devotional reading, use in worship, and sharing with others. The important thing is to feed yourself spiritually and learn from the wisdom and insights of others.

---

[22] "About the Center for Action and Contemplation," Center for Action and Contemplation, https://cac.org/about/who-we-are/.

[23] Martin Luther King Jr., *Why We Can't Wait* (New York: Harper & Row, 1963, 1964).

[24] Howard Thurman, *Jesus and the Disinherited* (New York, Nashville: Abingdon-Cokesbury Press, 1949).

[25] Gabby Cudjoe-Wilkes and Andrew Wilkes, *Psalms for Black Lives: Reflections for the Work of LIberation* (Nashville: Upper Room Books, 2022).

[26] Cole Arthur Riler, *Black Liturgies: Prayers, Poems and Meditations for Staying Human* (New York, Convergent Books, 2024).

[27] Kate Bowler and Jessica Richie, *The Lives We Actually Have: 100 Blessings for Imperfect Days* (New York: Convergent Books, 2023).

For the record, I am also a huge fan of all kinds of Christian music, from gospel—including traditional, contemporary, hip-hop, and rap—to "contemporary Christian music," classical music, music theater, and any kind of music that fills my soul. Feed yourself and your spirit well. It is at the heart of the Christian life and is the foundation from which we can be the followers of Christ we say we are.

The Danger of Religious Institutionalism

One of the challenges of any organized religion is facing the realities that association in organized religious bodies has been declining for decades. I was recently asked at a fairly large congregation, "So, are we growing? I heard that we should be trying to grow by 10 percent each year." I had to stop and take a breath. I was being confronted by a particular church growth strategy this man had heard once upon a time and somehow believed was the answer to the vitality of the church. Although Jesus gave the great commission to send us forth to go into all the world and make disciples, the institutions we have created were never outlined—nor do I believe Jesus ever imagined or intended the human religious institutions of modern Western Christianity. It is no secret that mainline denominational membership has been declining for decades. And far too many are still looking for the growth formula that will bring people into the building. Too many of us are seeking to prop up institutions that may no longer be relevant to the world we serve. Although size is one dimension of health, I am concerned that our focus is too often on how many members we have rather than the impact of our ministry on our communities, local society, and the world around us.

Churches are not merely 501(c)3 organizations. The leveraging of the nonprofit tax-exempt status by U.S. churches in particular has benefits and allows for a form of separation between church and state in terms of how finances are monitored. Beyond that, it ensures the freedom to worship and serve as we choose.

In Protestant denominations, church polity may follow either a congregational polity—in which each congregation is self-governing, calls its own pastors, and owns its own property and other resources—

or an episcopal form of governance, in which middle judicatory leaders, often called bishops, have the authority to appoint pastors and the denomination has the authority to assess congregations in order to provide support for the denomination. Every church and denomination is a human system; and, depending on how authority is derived, those in Western culture often have an unhealthy relationship with authority.

Whether the system is centralized or decentralized (as in congregational polity), many find themselves seeking the best way to maximize their own authority or minimize the authority of others over them. So often, resistance to change in any organization comes from those who benefit from the current system. It is deep relationship with God that equips us to be the church we say we are. Christians around the world frame their understanding of mission and Christian discipleship with words that usually include love, mission, service, justice, unity, and a call to bear witness to the good news of Jesus Christ. Spiritually dry people operate solely from their own understanding of organizational intentions. Yes, we need committees and boards and executives; but we also need a heart for God, the church of Jesus Christ, and the work Christians are called to do.

Having been in senior leadership for many years in both corporate America and higher education, I understand the dynamics of career planning, "ladder-climbing," and seeking favor with those who have more authority in the system. Unfortunately, there are clergy who see the church organization as a ladder to be climbed. Some may be more concerned about what their next promotional step is—not for the sake of living into their ministry but for the purpose of reaching a particular level in the church hierarchy—because they believe that represents professional success.

It is certainly important to live out your call in ever-increasingly fulfilling ways. We all want to grow and develop, to have new experiences. But in the church of Jesus Christ, our motivations must be to live into the call of Jesus to love God and neighbor and to share the good news, making disciples and bearing witness to God's limitless love. If we are not grounded theologically and spiritually in ways that impact how we live into the call, a quest for authority and prominence can distort how we understand our ministry.

We certainly need healthy leadership in the church, leaders who understand how to faithfully exercise authority and honor and develop the gifts in the body of Christ. But we must guard against being more concerned about the religious institutions from which we serve than we are about the ministry we say we practice. Preserving the institution for the sake of holding up human authority is a false understanding of what God has called us to. If we are not grounded spiritually, we fall prey to the human temptation for self-promotion. We need vital congregations and institutions to do effective ministry, but let us always hold first to the goal of being faithful to the teachings of Jesus, not just to the latest organizational development theory of how to build and keep institutions. Let us ground ourselves in the teachings of Jesus, informed by scriptural texts and nourished by deep spiritual practice. Only through such discipline can we find the strength and courage to truly be the church we say we are.

REFLECTION

1. What spiritual practices do you have for yourself? Your family? What kinds of practices are encouraged in your congregation?

2. How did you develop these practices? What value do they have for your life and that of your family? How might spiritual discipline aid in our mission to our community and world?

3. Name some scriptures that are meaningful to you. Is there a text that is a "theme scripture" or one you revisit often to encourage or comfort yourself?

4. Do you have a community in which you can study the Bible faithfully and critically, engaging and wrestling with difficult issues? How might you participate in such a community if you could?

5. How would you suggest that someone begin to develop his or her personal spiritual practices?

6. What kinds of Christian education are offered in your congregation?

7. Think about a time when prayer and scripture helped you during a difficult time in your life, or a time when you offered prayers of thanksgiving, and scripture gave you words to share that thanksgiving.

8. How does your tradition celebrate the Lord's Supper? What are the advantages of that tradition? What disadvantages do you see, if any?

9. If the Lord's table is also a metaphor for the community of God beyond the meal we celebrate, what should we be doing to bring this hospitality for all?

Staying at the Table

Then he took a loaf of bread, and when he had given thanks he broke it and gave it to them, saying, "This is my body, which is given for you. Do this in remembrance of me." And he did the same with the cup after supper, saying, "This cup that is poured out for you is the new covenant in my blood." (Luke 22:19–20; see also Mark 14:22–26)

For I received from the Lord what I also handed on to you, that the Lord Jesus on the night when he was betrayed took a loaf of bread, and when he had given thanks, he broke it and said, "This is my body that is for you. Do this in remembrance of me." In the same way he took the cup also, after supper, saying, "This cup is the new covenant in my blood. Do this, as often as you drink it, in remembrance of me." (1 Corinthians 11:23–25)

Christians all over the world share the meal that we call the Lord's supper, communion, or the eucharist (I will use these terms interchangeably to refer to the practice of sharing the bread and cup at the Lord's table). The passages cited are the source for what are known as "the words of institution," referring to the act of Jesus establishing this meal as a way for Christians to remember his salvific work on the cross.

The Christian Church (Disciples of Christ) came into being as a movement in the early nineteenth century in the United States largely because of systems of authority that restricted who could have access to the Lord's supper and who made those determinations. Our movement's founders—Alexander Campbell and Barton Stone—both disagreed with the communion practices of itinerant Presbyterian ministers. One was required to meet with a minister and receive a token if it was determined that one was worthy in that week to receive communion.

Campbell and Stone, among others at the time, felt that other human beings were not the ones who should be evaluating anyone's worthiness to receive this sacred meal. From that concern, the theology of the open table ultimately came to be articulated. Disciples believe that all are welcome at the Lord's table and that no one has the right to decide who may receive communion. It is not our table, we say, but the Lord's.

In most Disciples congregations, the Lord's supper is celebrated every Sunday and even in ministry board meetings, retreat, and camp settings. Communion is celebrated as a regular part of any event when the church is gathered. You need not be an ordained clergy to preside at the table, for we believe it is a believer's meal. Children and youth learn how to preside at the table at camp and other activities. In an invitation to the table during a worship service, it is usually stressed that, while it is a believer's meal, we ask no questions and turn no one away from being served. Across Christendom, Disciples are known for their regular celebration of the Lord's supper. The Bible references the frequency only as "as often as you do it."

But it is not the frequency that distinguishes the Disciples' theology of the table. It is the access that we believe is open to all. This access extends beyond the meal we celebrate at the table. Our welcome is intended to include all who wish to be a part of our congregations and communities. Our identity statement says quite plainly: "We welcome all to the Lord's Table as God has welcomed us."

I will be the first to admit that we still have a way to go to be the church that we say we are. While most Disciples congregations do take the Lord's supper every Sunday, practices vary across congregations: some celebrate only once a month, once a quarter, or even once a year. Some congregations believe that children who have not been baptized should not partake, for it is a believer's meal. But many congregations never ask those questions and allow anyone who approaches the table or anyone to whom a tray of the elements is passed to partake.

The Lord's supper is an important part of Disciples' worship. Many Christian traditions vary in their understanding of what actually happens at the table. For some, the bread or crackers literally become the body of Christ and the juice or wine literally becomes the blood of Jesus. For others, including Disciples, the elements of bread and wine—or, as we often say, the bread and cup—are symbols of the saving acts of Jesus on the cross. The power of the Holy Spirit makes Jesus present with us at the table. It is, indeed, Jesus' table; he is the host, and we are merely ushering others in to share. The radical welcome that is at the heart of our practice is not just an invitation to a meal; rather, it represents the covenant that Jesus establishes with all humankind at the table, inviting all to be in perpetual fellowship and communion with God.

Many Christian denominations require that only ordained clergy preside or even handle the communion elements of bread and cup (juice or wine). For those traditions that do not recognize women or anyone in the LGBTQ+ community as clergy, those who can officiate are further limited. Some Christian traditions allow only those who are part of their tradition to partake, whether they are believers in Christ in another tradition or not.

The World Council of Churches (WCC) is an ecumenical fellowship of Christian denominations and associations from all across the Protestant traditions. I currently serve as a member of the Central Committee, the primary deliberative body of the WCC. At a Central Committee meeting, a question for discussion was given to each small discussion group: What action could be taken to best exemplify and promote Christian unity? My response: Let's all share communion together.

But the reality is that, even in the World Council of Churches—the largest fellowship of Christian churches in the world—sharing the Lord's supper is something that cannot be done because there are such varying positions as to who may partake and who may preside or officiate, how the service might flow. Some traditions do not allow nonmembers to partake. Some traditions allow only clergy credentialed in the tradition to officiate. Some traditions have strict protocols about how the bread and cup are prepared. Some traditions do not recognize me, a woman, as clergy to begin with. It is a sad reality that the very meal Jesus taught us to share in order to remember his death and suffering is something that humanly derived doctrinal positions prevent us all from sharing together.

It is a bold statement to say that all are welcome at the Lord's table. When you say *all*, you must be committed to mean *all*. We know that at that original Lord's supper, Jesus was gathered with his twelve disciples, all of whom were Jewish. They were actually gathered for what they thought would be the traditional Passover meal. But Jesus took the elements of bread and wine and began to imbue this meal with new significance, teaching about what would happen in just a few short hours. This meal was to be a way for them to remember him, his death and suffering. Ultimately, Jesus knew they would celebrate this meal with the knowledge of his resurrection.

Seated at that table were men (no women in that time), most of them members of the working or artisan class, and not all of them got along. There were ambitious ones, like James and John, whose mother had lobbied Jesus for a place of prominence for her sons once Jesus established the earthly kingdom they all had anticipated. Peter, both a leader and one with a temper, was there. John—the disciple "whom Jesus loved," according to the Gospel of John—is often pictured in artists' renderings as being physically close to Jesus. Also at the table was Judas, the treasurer of the group, who would betray Jesus.

Like any group of coworkers or co-laborers, I'm sure there were things they each disliked about the other. Some were fishermen and carpenters; one was a tax collector. All of them had grown up in a Jewish world in which their land was dominated by the oppression of the Roman Empire. Jesus did not shun any of the twelve at the table. He did speak of someone at the table betraying him, and he told Judas to do what he was going to do quickly. Jesus' example of his relationships with the twelve teaches us that, regardless of the background or behavior of each one of the disciples, none was kept from sharing in the Lord's supper.

An invitation to the Lord's table is an act of the most radical hospitality. The table represents the community of God and the fellowship and covenant we have with God through Jesus. We choose not to limit who may receive. We choose not to examine one another to determine if we've been good enough that week to partake—for it is at the invitation of the Lord that we are called to remember at the table. One of the greatest gifts of my church is this commitment to the open table. And yet it is also one of our greatest challenges in being the church we say we are. Congregational polity allows that each congregation may celebrate as it chooses. Congregations have the freedom to determine who may partake, who may prepare the meal, and who may serve. Congregations are free even to determine who is welcome into their local worshiping communities.

So, given this freedom, how do we know that Jesus intended to include everyone? How do we know that we are not free to set our own rules as to who may be invited to the Lord's table? Jesus' words on the night of the Last Supper instituted what he called a new covenant in his blood. That covenant evokes the historical relationship of the covenant the God of Israel had throughout human history. God could be counted on to keep God's promises and covenant, and the law required certain compliance in order to access forgiveness and redemption. The new covenant that Jesus institutes is one that reorients those who would come to believe in Jesus toward a covenant in which God's limitless love continues to be available *not* because of works or other acts but through the saving acts of Jesus.

Christians can say all those words, and we can give beautiful invitations to the Lord's table and craft beautiful liturgies in all manner of traditions. But our failure to truly include all at the table is a sign of our wider failure to include all who would seek Jesus in our local communities, in our clergy and in our leadership. When we establish limits to access to the Lord's table, or to worship, or to participation in any ministry event, or to leadership and ordination, we deign to set limits that God does not set. The very idea that God is limited by our own theories and doctrines flies in the face of believing in a God whose authority, power, and—most of all—love is limitless. If left to our own devices, each of us might have different criteria for who we might want to be in our faith communities. We often have the audacity to decide for God whom God loves, accepts, and invites.

I reject the very notion that any of us can limit the God who is able to do far beyond all we can ask or think. Either God's love is limitless or God is not God. God's actions in history have demonstrated that, when humanity has failed to be true to God's law or to Jesus' teachings, God is always making a way for reconciliation. I do not think you can understand the commandment to love your neighbor as yourself and impose limits as to who is included.

Without spiritual depth and biblical grounding, we make our own choices based on our own wisdom. 1 Corinthians 1:25–28 is a passage I return to often, for it reminds us that God's foolishness is wiser than human wisdom. It is true that, based on our own behaviors, we make choices to experience more or less of God's love, but there is never any final exclusion from that love. And, most importantly, we are not the arbiters of whom God loves.

By our own decisions, we are drawing lines of exclusion. If you can draw a line, I get to draw one. And who knows whether our lines will actually wind up keeping ourselves from access to God? How can we try to prevent others from receiving the grace and love that we so freely have received from God?

Bishop Yvette Flunder, pastor of the City of Refuge United Church of Christ and presiding prelate of the Fellowship of Affirming Ministries, once said in a sermon, and I paraphrase here, "Our job is not to decide who may come to the Lord's table. Our job is to make sure that there are enough chairs for all who wish to come." I quote her on this in many an invitation to the Lord's table because it epitomizes not only the radical welcome but the active role we are called to take in making room for all.

"Having a seat at the table" is often a metaphor used to reflect inclusion to places where decisions are made and power is exercised. At the table of the Lord, there are no power structures, simply disciples of Jesus gathered to remember and be nourished and empowered for the work we are called to do. In predominantly White denominations, some have embraced the call to ensure that diverse voices of all identities are at the Lord's table, but they may or may not have moved to include all voices at the table of decision and power. The danger is in operating from a perspective that assumes that this is "our" table, that it is "our" church, or that the dominant culture still "owns" the table and who sits at it.

So many fractures within the body of Christ have resulted from divisions over various elements of theology or doctrine. Christians in various groups within denominations have decided that their perspective is the right one and everyone else should agree. When Christians have made a decision to leave their church denomination because of a theological disagreement, such actions not only harm religious institutions, they harm the very cause of Christ.

Throughout history, so many variations on the Christian understanding have developed into separation of ministries and denominations. Disagreements on slavery, the role of women in ministry, and the inclusion of LGBTQ+ persons have led to painful fractures. Such divisions are still happening in the twenty-first century. It is difficult for most of us to work alongside people with whom we disagree. But again, I return to the belief that we do not have the authority to supersede God and decide whom God includes and whom God loves.

Jesus never taught that there were any limitations on who was included as our neighbor. In fact, the parable of the good Samaritan intentionally uses a member of a group with which the Jews did not get along in order to make the point that *everyone* is our neighbor. Jesus' teachings often were not received as warmly because they challenged cultural norms that established a hierarchy of human worth. Such hierarchies still exist in the twenty-first century. In John 6, Jesus is trying to speak about his coming death and foreshadows the Lord's Supper by saying that they will eat his flesh and drink his blood. The disciples respond to what Jesus is saying by acknowledging that his teachingsare hard to receive and, perhaps, harder to live up to. I like the King James translation here:

> *These things said he in the synagogue, as he taught in Capernaum. Many therefore of his disciples, when they had heard this, said,* **This is a hard saying; who can hear it?** *When Jesus knew in himself that his disciples murmured at it, he said unto them, Doth this offend you? What and if ye shall see the Son of man ascend up where he was before? It is the spirit that quickeneth; the flesh profiteth nothing: the words that I speak unto you, they are spirit, and they are life. But there are some of you that believe not. For Jesus knew from the beginning who they were that believed not, and who should betray him. And he said, Therefore said I unto you, that no man can come unto me, except it were given unto him of my Father. From that time many of his disciples went back,* **and walked no more with him.** (John 6:59-66, emphasis added)

Jesus' teachings were not embraced by all those who followed. The source of their disagreement is not articulated, but they obviously did not believe in the authority of who Jesus was or what he was teaching. These were those beyond just the twelve who listened and often followed Jesus across the countryside. Some actually "walked no more with him." Jesus then engages the core twelve to see what they are thinking and feeling. And he knows that one of them will betray him (again, I am quoting the King James translation here):

> *Then said Jesus unto the twelve, Will ye also go away? Then Simon Peter answered him, Lord, to whom shall we go? thou hast the words of eternal life. And we believe and are sure that thou art that Christ, the Son of the living God. Jesus answered them, Have not I chosen you twelve, and one of you is a devil? He spake of Judas Iscariot the son of Simon: for he it was that should betray him, being one of the twelve.* (John 6:67–71)

It is not Jesus who sends the others away; they choose to go of their own volition. Peter affirms who they believe Jesus to be. Those who left could not accept the "hard sayings." They do not stay to engage or ask questions; they just leave.

Christian unity is a stated goal of many denominations, like my own, and of many ecumenical bodies, such as the National Council of Churches and the World Council of Churches. We speak of the "visible unity" of the church, and we pray that our work together is a powerful witness to who Jesus is and how the world might be different because of him. But none of these entities is able to avoid theological or social issues on which there is disagreement, and most often the strategy is to avoid discussion or positions in areas where there is disagreement so as to preserve the coalition. My own tradition understands unity to be a gift from God, something that is available for us to live into by choice. It is not something that is a human achievement or the result of successful negotiations. One chooses to live into Christian unity because one has first acknowledged the sovereignty of God—the lordship of Jesus Christ—and that such discipleship requires us to love God and our neighbor. It requires that we do not obstruct or reject the presence of anyone else, whether it be in our congregations and communities or at the Lord's table.

What does it mean to stay at the table? What does it mean to be committed to making room for all in our congregations and communities? We first acknowledge that, although we do not always agree, none of us has the right to bar the presence of the other. It is the table of the Lord, the church of Jesus Christ—it is God's creation. We are called to obedience to God's love just as the rest of creation is called. When we disagree, how do we respond? Circling our wagons and going home serves only to reinforce negative impressions that nonbelievers have about the hypocrisy of the church. How are we any "better" if we cannot practice what Jesus teaches?

As I quoted earlier, my home pastor, Dr. Tom Benjamin, had a mantra he taught to the children in the church: "We do not have to agree, but I must respect you and you must respect me." Such respect for one another is grounded in our understanding that all are created in the image of God, that all have worth, and that we are commanded to love our neighbor as ourselves and to love one another as Jesus has loved us. This is the root declaration by which all else must be measured. Your inability to respect me does not give you permission to remove me from the kin[g]dom of God, let alone from the Lord's table. You do not have the right to sanction my destruction because you disagree with what I say, what I believe, or who I am. I cannot say it enough: we just don't have the right to diminish those whom God loves.

I certainly acknowledge that across so many church traditions there is disagreement about who is welcome, not just at the Lord's table but in the community of God. The question must be asked: What happens when we disagree on the very basic tenet that all are welcome at the table? I believe that if we begin with a foundation of God as a God of limitless love, we cannot arrive at a conclusion that we should deny anyone. The very idea that any one of us has the authority to deny any of us presupposes that there is a group who has the primary authority. It is the table of the Lord, and Jesus is the host. The radical welcome of God's limitless love places God's covenant at the center.

Sadly, we see congregations and other groups within Christianity being fractured over this basic premise. I cannot relent on this foundational belief. If any of us can limit whom God loves or welcomes, God is no longer the limitless God of limitless love. And although we may resist division on every hand, we must also stand firmly for the radical welcome of all. If you disagree, I would love to discuss this with you. But as for me, to borrow from Reformation leader Martin Luther: "Here I stand; I can do no other."

As a Black woman of a certain age, I am familiar with not being welcome in many spaces. I have experience with those who are not of my heritage assuming that my background means that I am not equipped to hold certain roles. The way I speak, the way I move, the way I dress, the style I use in worship—these are often deemed by many to be inferior because they are different from their own experience. In American society, the insidious presence of racism has meant that there are assumptions that quality, success, and excellence tied to White societal norms. There is also the assumption, fueled by Christian nationalists, that the only American religion is Christianity and that the only way to be a "good" American is to be Christian.

Similarly, Christian nationalists believe that the only kind of faithful Christian is one who accepts a particular ideology of American exceptionalism. Anyone who does not fit this mold is not valued, not the right kind of Christian … not the right kind of American.

Many people, including me, disagree vehemently with those views. There are those who claim to be Christian who will go to the wall arguing that women are not fit to serve in ministry because, they claim, the Bible says that women are not to teach or speak. The arguments used to limit who is at the table are usually based on a particular interpretation of scripture. "It's in the Bible," people say.

We must consider of any biblical text: How does it speak to the message of God's limitless love? If the lens that is used does not affirm the limitless love of God for all, such interpretations violate the love of God. The "clobber passages"—scriptures that are used to argue against the acceptance, indeed the humanity, of those who are part of the LGBTQ+ community—are additional examples of scriptures that are misinterpreted and used in abusive ways against those whose humanity is beloved to God and should therefore be beloved to any who claim to love God and follow Jesus.

Passages from the epistles of Paul were used to justify the enslaving of Africans, and the misreading of a supposed curse placed upon Noah's son Ham are further examples of how some people have been marginalized by Christians who wield their own scriptural interpretations as a weapon against their neighbors. When all are welcome, when we claim to love God and our neighbor, and when we commit to following the way of Jesus, we must stay at the table and argue to the end that all of those who may be different or with whom we may disagree have a place at that same table.

Those who have historically been denied a place at the table are also obliged to stay at the table, even though their presence has been denied in the past. Many persons in these groups have asked me, "Terri, how can I stay at the table when the seat I am in is a thorny seat?" "What if I strongly disagree with someone else's biblical interpretation or theology?" "What if those at the table hold beliefs that are an assault to my humanity? How can I be at that table?" I fully understand such concerns. My own identity has made the seat I take at many tables uncomfortable. Sometimes it is important to choose another table when one feels that one's humanity is being assaulted or that one is not safe. You may be fully confident in the fact that God loves you, and yet you may not feel safe at certain tables. You have the right to choose another table in another vineyard.

It is important for us to remember that we all have a seat and it is by the invitation of Jesus. There are congregations that do not affirm women in ministry, do not accept LGBTQ+ persons, and would rather not embrace people of color in the congregations. If we do not also see the witness of congregations that are committed to full welcome and inclusion, we risk eternal damage to some of God's beloved. It is not God who hurts and excludes people; it is people claiming to love God but deciding that they will exclude others that cause hurt. You do not have to agree or even understand—and you may actually believe that who people identify themselves to be is against scripture—but none of us has the right to limit whom God loves.

When we can show the world that the body of Christ is more concerned about bearing witness to God's limitless love than we are about who is right on any point of doctrine, we make a powerful witness. In John 17, Jesus prays for those who will come to believe because of the witness of those first twelve disciples. He prays for unity not as a feel-good "kumbayah" moment, but as a way to show the world that God truly sent Jesus. Then the world will believe that God loves and welcomes them and that the people of God care more about that truth than anything else. I have stressed the importance of understanding what we believe about God, committing to the way of love, engaging in deepening our spiritual disciplines, especially prayer and contemplative practice and the study of scripture. Without this kind of theological and spiritual grounding, we are merely members of a human organization who privilege our own opinions and perpetuate a narrative that says those who are already here are the ones whose voices are most important." An invitation to the table cannot mean that I'm welcome only if I agree with your perspective. It cannot mean that we see others as being invited to have a place at *our* table.

A Context of Division and Polarization

The social climate in the United States has become increasingly polarized in recent decades. Many believe that Christians should have nothing to say about the civil government or even critique the government. Although religious nonprofits cannot endorse candidates, the very role of the prophet is not only to critique the empire but to cast a vision of the alternate society that is possible because of Jesus' teachings and vision for the kin[g]dom of God. Some of our divisions are rooted in a commitment to tradition; but, as I have noted above, that commitment often is more to the traditions of institutions rather than to the way of Jesus and the promise of the gospel of Jesus Christ. Some polarization is the classic tension between generations. Many of us who are "of a certain age" forget that we were once the youth and young adults who had new ideas and who pushed against traditions we felt were no longer relevant. But some of the polarization we encounter is grounded in our placing other belief systems above our understanding of the gospel. When we cannot change, we cannot grow.

One of the gifts of the COVID-19 pandemic was that we were forced to do things differently, to learn new ways of being together, be it online worship or online giving. Doing it the way it had been done was not an option, and in these pandemic-informed times, we know that there is no return to what was. One of the learnings I had was about the importance of building the capacity for change in our communities.

Change can be emotionally and psychologically challenging, especially when change is necessitated because of a disaster or pandemic or other factors beyond our control. Many companies begin and know success because of an innovative product or process they bring to the market. Ultimately, that product or service may become obsolete due to technology shifts or changes in cultural norms. Work life since the pandemic has shifted greatly, and workers are demanding more control over the quality of their work experience. Many people had time to reflect on what they really wanted from life and work, and they made life-changing decisions as a result. Companies must always have an eye toward understanding how needs are changing so that they can be prepared to offer products that are relevant in shifting times. Organizations that do not build within themselves a capacity to look forward, to anticipate change, and to embrace change as a natural part of growth are doomed to pass from the scene. People in those organizations also need to develop tools for dialogue and discourse.

The same is true with the body of Christ. When we allow that the Holy Spirit is always speaking, that God always has a relevant word for the current moment, we can have the courage to change, to give ourselves permission to be free from the fear of what happens when we do. We cannot be afraid to let go of what no longer works.

We cannot be blind to the realities that younger generations do not form attachments to institutions like the church in the way that prior generations did. Volumes of data remind us that the percentage of those who do not affiliate with any religious tradition—the so-called "nones"—is now the largest percentage of the population.

Now that many congregations offer livestreaming of their worship services, some people are opting not to return to in-person services as often. Even older members are finding it more convenient and often safer to worship online. We cannot now denigrate the online experience because we want everyone back in the pews. We must see the shift and develop new approaches to minister to those folks who worship from home. Developing the role of an "e-pastor" who engages with those online during worship and is attentive to their needs and concerns is being used by many congregations to minister to a growing number of people who choose to worship online.

Instead of ignoring those people and deciding that we can't serve them if they don't come to the building, congregations are developing Christian education offerings, prayer times, even counseling with a pastor online. Many pastors will tell me that they have people from across the United States, Canada, and even around the world worshiping with them on Sundays. I would venture that many of these new worshipers may not have chosen or even had the opportunity to enter their doors. We have tremendous opportunities for ministry by engaging our online worshipers and creating points of contact that were simply not possible or even necessary before.

Let me remind you of the important changes my church is making to create greater connection across the whole denomination and encourage deeper engagement with the decision-making processes of our life together as church. One of the important shifts is now possible because of technology and is being embraced in large part because of the lessons learned during the pandemic. We have been able to imagine a way of gathering and sharing that we probably could not have thought possible before the pandemic. A structure that places a high value on the participation of every congregation must decide to empower that participation and commit to the fullest range of accessibility and participation. We want to provide more access to the decision-making process and reduce the economic barriers to that access presented by the cost of living and travel. We want to give more time to discussion and discernment, not just the up or down vote on a list of business items. More time together and more access to the process will create new pathways to engagement. Digital devices for voting will give greater agency to all congregations. Local gatherings will be connected online to the wider denominational gathering, with all being invited to listen, speak, and share, whether you are a voting delegate or not.

We are imagining a more engaged church in which more people have access to the conversations and information that shape decisions in the life of the church. Had the pandemic not occurred, the comfort level with such technology would likely not be there. Although it is still a major cultural shift in terms of how we do business, there is excitement about the opportunity to be a part of conversations and decisions. By enacting these changes, we are building a capacity for the future to continue to imagine new ways of ministry and new understandings of God's call on us, and we are providing opportunities for all of us to learn how to engage in discourse that is not only civil but welcoming.

Additionally, the General Board will move from being merely a group of representatives from regional and general ministries with only a few at-large members to a smaller board that is curated from nominations across the life of the church. We want to identify clergy and laity who have a variety of gifts that the church needs as it prioritizes mission, stewards its resources, and continues to think about how we organize ourselves as a covenantal body. These changes will take time, and the processes will continue to evolve.

My hope and confidence is in the God who is able to do far beyond all we can ask or think. If God's imagination is limitless, so are our possibilities as the people of God. Capacity for change must be a core competency that we build into the life of every congregation. Not being afraid to change if something doesn't work gives us an understanding that moving forward together is possible. God has given us God's limitless possibilities, and God invites us to discover all that is possible if we only believe. We cannot move forward in fear; instead, we must move forward trusting in the ability of God to see us forward. If you believe in a God of limitless possibilities, this is not just fluff. It is a testament to the power of the God we serve.

REFLECTION

1. What words of vision and strategy are present in your tradition? Do these words inspire you for discipleship?

2. What limitations do you see in the institutional structure in your tradition? How might you imagine change either for your tradition or for all of Christianity?

3. What are the biggest challenges you face in creating great connection across your church/denominational community?

4. How does your tradition deal with disagreement and conflict? Who participates in decision-making at the congregational level? How are decisions made at the denominational level?

5. How might a Christian community foster an environment where those who may disagree with some aspect of theology or practice still feel welcome? Does your tradition make allowance for such disagreement? If so, how? If not, what do you think of that position?

Changing the Narrative

Christians everywhere are seeking ways to "revitalize," "transform," and even reimagine what it means to be a community of faith. Leaders are asking how we can address congregational vitality, even as there are congregations whose viability is at risk. We have moved from a strategy of planting more new churches to teaching existing congregations how to operate from the same innovative vantage point that new congregations have always been encouraged to have. In multicultural denominations like mine, our commitment to anti-racism continues to be a challenge. We have been doing anti-racism training for years, but it has not yet really integrated into congregational life beyond being a requirement for clergy continuing education. Denominations have struggled with divisions over culture and social issues, resulting in denominational splits. Even when a denomination has not split, there are still many cases of congregations leaving over these divisions.

We often use the word "transformation" to describe activities and programs that can address congregational vitality. But it is hard to know exactly what the end game of transformation is. Are we transformed because we went through a curriculum over a two-day retreat? Are we transformed because we have made commitments to participate in social action for justice on a few occasions? Are we transformed because we restructure congregational boards and implement new models of Christian education?

My perspective on how transformation must happen was revolutionized through a conversation about six years ago with Rev. Dr. David Anderson Hooker, a minister/lawyer/peace studies professor/conflict management consultant. I met Dr. Hooker at a National Council of Churches event aligned with its anti-racism initiative. I wanted to talk about how we could reimagine the work of anti-racism to go beyond clergy training and make it a more integral part to who we understand ourselves to be. We had named the priority; we just needed to think about how to do it differently. However, Dr. Hooker's conversation led me to understand that this was not just a matter of our anti-racism initiative. There were likely elements of our existing unspoken narrative that were keeping us from being who we say we are in many other ways. He helped me understand that unless the church addressed its underlying narrative, we would not be able to live into our priority of being an anti-racist church.

Dr. Hooker asked me a question that shifted my perspective: "Did you ever name what the church would look like, what it would feel like when you became an anti-racist church?" Through his work on the power of narrative, as we talked further he explained that we could do all the training in the world, but if we had not changed the narrative into which we live, nothing would really change. We discussed how we might explore existing narrative, build the capacity for the church to name the problem, and identify an alternate narrative that would be based on what we wanted the church to look like, feel like, and how we wanted people to experience our denomination, no matter what congregation they were in. In several meetings, online workshops with leaders across our church, Dr. Hooker helped to name the importance of narrative and illuminate the difference between narratives and stories.

We each have stories, and the narrative is the unspoken rules by which we align our stories to the greater whole. Dr. Hooker uses the metaphor of cars and highways. The stories are the cars, and the narrative is the highway. The highway dictates where you can go, how fast, and when and where you exit. Our stories are the cars. We may allow many different cars onto the highway, but even when more and diverse cars are allowed, they are still limited by the existing highway as to where they can go. Only by building a new highway or narrative can we address the complex problems in our existing narratives by building a preferred narrative of our shared future.

Inherent in these narratives are the kinds of power that are intrinsic to narratives. Constraining power keeps us in alignment with the existing narrative, and we make choices because we unconsciously understand that certain options are not available to us, or that we have a particular place or role in the system. Productive power "influences people's actions by directing them to act in certain ways whether those actions are serving their best interests or not."[28]

The preferred narrative is one that is derived from honest analysis of the problem and a teasing out of what we want the church to look like, feel like, actually be like. The future is shared because we are all empowered to help create it. We are all at the table, and we have named and removed unspoken understandings of who or what group may have controlled the shaping and policing of the current narrative. The Transformative Community Conferencing[29] (TCC) process was offered by Dr. Hooker as a way to guide the work. We call our work within the Disciples the Church Narrative Project.

The TCC process as we have used it usually is structured as follows: diverse voices from across a particular population are invited to attend a one-and-a-half-day event. It is important that a variety of perspectives are included in the work, just as a diversity of voices is important in any kind of ministry, imagining, or decision-making. We are doing TCCs region by region. As of this writing, fifteen of our thirty-one regions have participated, and by the time this book is in your hands, two or three more regions will have joined them. We have learned that the dynamic is very different when it is a clergy-only group versus a group that includes laity, and we believe that a mixture of clergy and laity yields the most comprehensive analysis and outcome.

Storytelling starts our sessions. We invite six to eight people to share stories responding to a particular prompt. Prior to the TCC, a storytelling coach works with the storytellers to help them craft an effective telling of their stories. (Think "The Moth" story hour done in a church setting.) The storytellers are given the prompt: "Tell us about

---

[28] David Anderson Hooker, *The Little Book of Transformative Community Conferencing* (New York: Good Books, 2016), 43.

[29] *The Little Book of Transformative Community Conferencing* articulates the TCC process for engaging in the development of a preferred narrative of a shared future. You will find more a in-depth discussion of what I'm sharing here in this book.

a time when you had an 'aha' moment." The stories need not have anything to do with church or faith. The storytelling creates a sense of community and shared vulnerability as we hear from others and even see ourselves in their stories. What emerges is always some unknown detail about the storyteller. Other participants are invited to write a short response to a prompt on small slips of paper that are read to the group in between the stories. We livestream the storytelling so that people across the church can be a part of the event. The storytelling is certainly a rich element of the TCC process, but it is not by any means the core of the process.

After the storytelling, Dr. Hooker begins by using a movie clip, then invites us to name the problems in the clip. At the heart of this process is the belief that, as Dr. Hooker says, "people are not the problem, the problem is the problem." Invariably, people will express skepticism about the veracity of this principle, as we all know people we consider to be problems. As we discuss the mapping of problems in the clip, we are asked: "If people are *not* the problem and the problem is the problem, how would you name the problem you saw in the movie?" As people respond, the facilitator creates a map using a flipchart, writing down all the things that people notice are "problems" in the movie clip. They discuss whether the problem stems from a situation or context that is beyond what they were able to see. By using this movie clip and learning how to name and recognize the problem in the situation, we have been introduced to the mapping process we will apply to the church the next day. It is important that we learn how to externalize the problem so that it is not tied to any person or group of people.

The next day, mapping the problem is done in small groups with the help of a facilitator. On easel paper, the facilitator draws a circle. As people name the problems, they are written on the paper as either core problems (inside the circle) or symptoms of the problem (outside the circle). We've found that sometimes church folks are what some have called "church nice" and are hesitant to name problems when there are other clergy or church members in the room. Part of the major breakthroughs that have happened have come when we see the conversation moving toward an honest naming of the problems, which may be related to people's congregations, regions, or the wider church. We often hear about the pain points that impact our congregations and regions, and we learn about communications issues as people are often not as connected or informed as we'd like to think, despite our best efforts. The mapping is not a gripe session but an honest analysis of what really ails the church. Dr. Hooker offers that "when participants map problematics, they are simultaneously identifying the effective contours of both *constraining* and *productive* power in dominant community and organizational narratives."[30] In several sessions, feedback has been that it was the most honest conversation we've held in a while; in one region, long suppressed issues of tension were surfaced and discussed. One regional minister spoke of the Church Narrative Project this way: "Miracles happened. I pray it catches fire across the whole church."

Using the map of the problem, the facilitator uses the words on the page to summarize the dominant narrative that has been outlined. As that summary is heard, there are often sounds of agreement, nodding heads, and usually a sense of amazement at seeing what they had named being reflected back to them. A part of the discussion may involve the question of how one or more of the problems is having a hidden impact in one's life.

The next step is the mapping of alternative narratives. What do we want the church to be like, act like, *feel* like? I'm always struck by the question of what we want the church to feel like because it allows us to speak to the fact that current dominant narratives may indeed be hurtful to many among us, and these very people are usually not the ones who hold the power in the dominant current narrative. As people share what they want the church to be like, what attributes they believe can counter the problems they have offered, I am always excited to hear in the conversation a great love for our church. People really do want their church, their denomination, to be a vibrant, transforming place. They have pride as they talk about what makes our denomination unique and why they have chosen to serve within

---

[30] Ibid., 43.

it. The process of naming the alternative preferred narrative is all the more powerful because we have spent time mapping the problems, so this step is grounded both in reality and in a belief that God is able to do what we imagine. We are reimagining our church, not a local civic club. Hope arises when we can tell the truth and then proceed to dream.

The facilitator then gives a summary of the elements of the alternate narrative. Without fail, at the end, people are smiling and saying, "Yes! That's the church we want."

After the TCC has concluded, participants in the regional session are invited to engage in an online debriefing. They will have access to the maps of their problems and the alternate preferred narrative. Within each region, volunteers are identified who want to be trained in the TCC process. We hope this process can be used across the life of the regions as a way of building capacity to name the problems and articulate alternative solutions. It is important to note that we do *not* see the Church Narrative Project merely as a series of TCC sessions, but we hope to leverage the process across the church, building the skills and capacity of many to be able to do this kind of analysis and visioning.

Our goal is to use the various mappings as a way to build from the ground a preferred narrative of our shared future as a church. In September 2024, representatives from twelve of the regions that had then completed a TCC gathered in a hotel in Chicago. As they walked into the meeting room, all of their problem maps and alternative narrative maps were posted around the room. During our time together, each region's representatives were given time to review and discuss their own maps. Next, there was time to review the whole gallery and make notes of comparison as they all reviewed each other's maps.

This was a session in which many said that they could begin to connect the dots and understand where the process was taking us. They saw clearly so many commonalities across the maps of both problematic and alternative narratives. They were also in a room with people from almost half the church's regions who had experienced the same process. I left that meeting full of excitement and hope. I felt that our work was starting to bear fruit and that we could continue the momentum as we worked with the rest of the regions.

The development of a new preferred narrative of a shared future will be developed from these mappings. Already, the commonalities are emerging, and the seeds are there to build the preferred narrative as we continue to work around the church. Imagining together can be energizing, and in it, we are finding great hope for what is possible.

One of the most powerful spiritual practices that Dr. Hooker has introduced to us is "Dayenu." Dayenu is the practice of declaring: "It would have been enough if God had only [fill in the blank], but God also [fill in the blank]." This is a practice of telling the story, bearing witness to God's goodness, and reminding ourselves of all that God has done *already*. If we can believe in not only the power but the sufficiency of God, our ability to believe that God is able to do far beyond all we can ask or imagine is strengthened. Dr. Hooker always asks the question, just as Jesus asked: "Can you just believe?"

One of the great encouragements that has come to us through the Church Narrative Project is Dr. Hooker's declaration to us: "The Disciples of Christ are small enough to change and big enough to change the world." May it be so.

When we began the Church Narrative Project, we were still in the discerning process about the governance changes that have now been approved and will be implemented effective immediately at the close of the 2025 General Assembly. From the beginning, I had shared with Dr. Hooker that I believed our work together would help to build capacity for a more engaged church membership. In our opening remarks at each TCC, both Dr. Hooker and I have continued to connect the dots so that it would be clear how this work relates to the other imaginings happening in the church. Having observed people engage in the often-delicate process of naming the problem and then watching them together allow themselves to imagine what an alternative narrative might look like, it is clear that those who have participated are building important skills for naming the truth and externalizing that truth so that it can be assessed critically and faithfully.

As we move to gather more frequently as the General Assembly, both online and in person, this experience has begun to generate a new skill set in our regions. I hope that those TCC participants will be more comfortable with naming a problem or issue and understanding that "people are not the problem, the problem is the problem." We are learning how an unspoken narrative may be crippling our future and that our ability to name an alternative narrative is imperative in order to be the church we say we are. As Walter Brueggemann reminds us, we can implement anything, but we must first engage in the imagining, the "futuring fantasy." I love watching people imagine together for the edification of the church.

The power of building capacity to sit with one another and tell the truth cannot be overestimated. Staying at the table requires honesty, candor, truth telling, but above all a commitment to engage with one another in the love that God has given to us. As you gaze around a room or a table, there may be people you don't like, people with whom you disagree, and people with whom you may have nothing in common, whether it be background, life experience, education, identity, political worldview, or even theological perspective. The ability to listen to opinions, thoughts, or experiences that are different from your own is an act of deep respect for the other. Our human instincts are to avoid engagement with those with whom we disagree or with those whose perspectives are harmful to our own sense of human dignity. We must get to the point at which people with very firmly held beliefs based on a particular interpretation of scripture are able to engage and not simply walk away. We have to hear from one another what we are thinking and feeling, and we have to be open to facing the realities of what our actions are doing to each other and how they may be keeping others from embracing the gathered church life that we offer. Truth telling is a necessary capacity that we must build.

But of course the truth must be spoken, for our lives depend on it, truth that subverts our best self-deceiving certitudes. The church has no monopoly on this vocation of *truth-telling*.

But *it is nonetheless the emancipatory vocation of the church.* And that vocation, as before Pharaoh and as before the Roman governor, is not welcome. It is unwelcome because the freedom it generates is scary, rather like living without a safety net. There are other voices of truth-telling as well; but the church is peculiarly defined by that task. And those who serve as truth-tellers in the church, like those who listen to the truth-telling in the church, are a mix of yearning and fearfulness, of receptiveness and collusion. In the end, the work of truth-telling is not to offer a new package of certitudes that displaces old certitudes. This truth to be uttered and acted, rather, is the enactment and conveyance of this Person who is truth, so that truth comes as bodily fidelity that stays reliably present to the pain of the world. Since the old Exodus, the truth has emerged in unexpected ways, from below. As an alternative to the alliance of power and truth that Foucault has so well chronicled, this evangelical offer of truth arises in a convergence of holy resolve and voiced pain, a convergence made echoingly available in the cry from the cross where human pain and divine purpose intersect.[31] (emphasis added)

Truth telling is "the emancipatory vocation" of the church. Wow, just wow! When we value being "nice" over telling the truth, we are out of step with the power of the the good news of Jesus Christ. Being truthful with ourselves and with one another helps us to both face and name what is missing, what is hurtful, what is keeping others from hearing our message. There is certainly no weakness in the gospel of Jesus Christ. But when we are living one thing while saying another, and when we deny the reality of powerful narratives that give dominance and power to one group and not to others, we are weakening the possibilities for reception of that good news. Such failure to face the truth creates the image of hypocrisy, generates hurt, and deepens divisions. In the American context, we have to be honest about how sociological injustices have made their imprint in the church and how power assumptions that are present in the secular world have

---

[31] Walter Brueggemann, *Truth-Telling as Subversive Obedience* (Eugene, OR: Cascade Books, 2011), 7.

invaded the church. We must name a problem to face a problem and find solutions that are liberating for everyone involved. Herein lies the power of building a preferred narrative of a shared future. It is not just sharing the building of the narrative, but it is building a preferred narrative of the future in which all will share justly.

As the church moves forward to implement a new vision, we must continue to tell the truth about what is working and what is not. We do not scrap entire ideas because a piece or step isn't working as we thought. We continue to focus on the purpose for the new vision and make the necessary adjustments to the plan. The ability to tell and receive the truth helps us to be more capable of being the loving people God has called us to be.

REFLECTION

1. Why is it important to consider what it will feel like or look like when our future vision becomes reality?

2. How comfortable are you or others in your community with naming the problems present in your context?

3. Do you agree with the theory that "people are not the problem, the problem is the problem"? If not, why? If so, how might this be helpful in imagining a future?

4. What barriers exist in your congregation or wider church community to naming the problem? In what ways are others around you resistant to shifting a narrative?

5. How do you understand the current narrative of your faith community? To what extent is it subconscious or unnamed?

6. What is the importance of narrative in how we live out our discipleship in community?

I Want a Church ...

In a pandemic-informed world in which the ideological and political polarizations of secular society have invaded the church; racism, misogyny, xenophobia, homophobia, and all manner of "isms" diminish the respect for people inside and outside of the church; and Christian nationalism distorts the message of Jesus Christ, is it any wonder the institutional church is declining in numbers?

Some Christians think the church should not speak on matters of public policy because "politics doesn't belong in the church." Although it is true that religious nonprofit organizations are legally prohibited from engaging in partisan support of political candidates, the Bible gives us clear instruction that the people of God and followers of Jesus are to hold the those in civil authority accountable for the just treatment of the least of these, be they poor, unhoused, or discriminated against because of any dimension of identity. Through the words of the Hebrew prophets; the apostles of the New Testament; and, most importantly, Jesus' own teachings, we have clear instructions as to our call to care for all and work for justice and flourishing for all whom God has created.

We have clear instruction not to neglect the widow or orphan. Widows historically were dependent on a male relative to provide for them after their husbands had died. If a widow had no such family support, she was doomed to live in poverty. There is consistent admonishment to not oppress "the resident alien" or "stranger," for the people of Israel were reminded that they were once strangers in Egypt. The care of widows, orphans, and strangers appears in several texts in the Hebrew Bible. Here are just two instances:

> *You shall not wrong or oppress a resident alien, for you were aliens in the land of Egypt. You shall not abuse any widow or*

orphan. If you do abuse them, when they cry out to me, I will surely heed their cry. (Exodus 22:21–23)

For the Lord your God is God of gods and Lord of lords, the great God, mighty and awesome, who is not partial and takes no bribe, who executes justice for the orphan and the widow, and who loves the strangers, providing them food and clothing. You shall also love the stranger, for you were strangers in the land of Egypt. (Deuteronomy 10:17–19)

Those who owned fields were commanded to give of their abundance so that it would be available for the stranger, the orphan, and the widow. Those who do so, scripture tells us, will be blessed in all their undertakings. In this practice, there is a clear understanding that those who have abundance are responsible to share what they have. No one is to hold all their abundance only for themselves. This is not a burden, for God will continue to bless them so they can continue to give in this way. Those who critique various social programs or safety nets for the poor violate God's commandment to love, expressed as a command to share what you have with those who have less.

When you reap your harvest in your field and forget a sheaf in the field, you shall not go back to get it; it shall be left for the alien, the orphan, and the widow, so that the Lord your God may bless you in all your undertakings. When you beat your olive trees, do not strip what is left; it shall be for the alien, the orphan, and the widow. When you gather the grapes of your vineyard, do not glean what is left; it shall be for the alien, the orphan, and the widow. Remember that you were a slave in the land of Egypt; therefore I am commanding you to do this. (Deuteronomy 24:19–22)

The call to do justice for the marginalized and oppressed is clear:

Learn to do good; seek justice; rescue the oppressed; defend the orphan; plead for the widow. (Isaiah 1:17)

Woe to those who make iniquitous decrees, who write oppressive statutes, to turn aside the needy from justice and to rob the poor of my people of their right, to make widows their spoil and to plunder orphans! (Isaiah 10:1–2)

Is not this the fast that I choose: to loose the bonds of injustice, to undo the straps of the yoke, to let the oppressed go free, and to break every yoke? Is it not to share your bread with the hungry and bring the homeless poor into your house; when you see the naked, to cover them and not to hide yourself from your own kin? (Isaiah 58:6–7)

Caring for the hungry and those who are oppressed and afflicted brings the blessings of God. Our needs will always be met, and our societies will be strong. Ensuring the flourishing of those in our society allows us to "raise up the foundations of many generations," for poverty and oppression can become systemic if it not addressed. We are called to "repair the breach" that exists in society.

If you offer your food to the hungry and satisfy the needs of the afflicted, then your light shall rise in the darkness and your gloom be like the noonday. The Lord will guide you continually and satisfy your needs in parched places and make your bones strong, and you shall be like a watered garden, like a spring of water whose waters never fail. Your ancient ruins shall be rebuilt; you shall raise up the foundations of many generations; you shall be called the repairer of the breach, the restorer of streets to live in. (Isaiah 58:10–12)

Christians often quote Micah 6:8 as a core teaching of the Hebrew Bible. But we must look at the verses that precede it to situate the prophet's admonition properly. It is not enough simply to give sacrifices or attend to rituals as they did in the ancient world. In the twenty-first century, we are often more focused on the production of our worship services than we are in living out the commandment to ensure justice in our world. God does not receive our rituals if our actions have not been consistent with the call to love and care for our neighbor—for all those who are oppressed and marginalized among us. Our worship means nothing to God if we are not faithful to his command:

"With what shall I come before the Lord and bow myself before God on high? Shall I come before him with burnt offerings, with calves a year old? Will the Lord be pleased with thousands of rams,

with ten thousands of rivers of oil? Shall I give my firstborn for my transgression, the fruit of my body for the sin of my soul?" He has told you, O mortal, what is good, and what does the Lord require of you but to do justice and to love kindness and to walk humbly with your God? (Micah 6:6-8)

Micah tells us that God has been very clear about what God requires. Dr. Lisa Davison, Hebrew Bible scholar and academic dean at Phillips Theological Seminary, offers my favorite translation of the words usually rendered as "do justice": *Make justice happen*. Justice is not simply a project; it is working toward a world in which all have enough, we all have dignity, we all know the love of God. When we love kindness and seek mercy, we are bearing witness to God's limitless love.

If I were to reorder this text, I would start with "walk humbly with your God." As I have repeated throughout this book, we are not prepared to truly be disciples of Jesus, to bear witness to God's limitless love, unless we are engaged in spiritual practices that allow us to know more intimately the presence of God and have the kind of relationship Jesus desired we would have with God. We must also be students of the biblical text, not as a source of dogmatic orthodoxy but as a way to prayerfully discern what God is saying in this time and how we are to continue to show the world what our society can be like because Jesus has come. As Christians, we must be known as those who seek a better world because we ourselves have experienced the transforming power of the love of God through Jesus Christ. People should want to be a part of our churches because they see among us something different, the transforming impact of Jesus that causes us to flout the norms of society that call for self-centeredness and acquisition of things and power. When people do not see that we have been changed, when they encounter the same structural injustice in the church that they see in the world, not only are we disobedient to God but we damage the very message of good news in Christ that we say is our primary concern.

We are perhaps more familiar with the teachings of Jesus in the New Testament. I have already shared Jesus' teachings on love. Now I want to share the words of Matthew 25, which epitomize how Jesus sees our obligation to care for our neighbors. Jesus says:

"When the Son of Man comes in his glory and all the angels with him, then he will sit on the throne of his glory. All the nations will be gathered before him, and he will separate people one from another as a shepherd separates the sheep from the goats, and he will put the sheep at his right hand and the goats at the left. Then the king will say to those at his right hand, 'Come, you who are blessed by my Father, inherit the kingdom prepared for you from the foundation of the world, for I was hungry and you gave me food, I was thirsty and you gave me something to drink, I was a stranger and you welcomed me, I was naked and you gave me clothing, I was sick and you took care of me, I was in prison and you visited me.'

"Then the righteous will answer him, 'Lord, when was it that we saw you hungry and gave you food or thirsty and gave you something to drink? And when was it that we saw you a stranger and welcomed you or naked and gave you clothing? And when was it that we saw you sick or in prison and visited you?' And the king will answer them, 'Truly I tell you, just as you did it to one of the least of these brothers and sisters of mine, you did it to me.'

"Then he will say to those at his left hand, 'You who are accursed, depart from me into the eternal fire prepared for the devil and his angels, for I was hungry and you gave me no food, I was thirsty and you gave me nothing to drink, I was a stranger and you did not welcome me, naked and you did not give me clothing, sick and in prison and you did not visit me.'

"Then they also will answer, 'Lord, when was it that we saw you hungry or thirsty or a stranger or naked or sick or in prison and did not take care of you?' Then he will answer them, 'Truly I tell you, just as you did not do it to one of the least of these, you did not do it to me.'" (Matthew 25:31–45)

When we serve and care for others among us, we are ministering to Jesus himself. If the command to simply love our neighbors just as Jesus has loved us is not sufficient for you, perhaps the idea that every person to whom you minister is indeed Jesus himself might cause you to reevaluate how you see others. I have said it before, and I'll say it again: we do not have the right to decide who God loves or who is worthy of our love. We are called to love as Jesus has loved us (John 13:34–35), and we are called to love God and neighbor—that "greatest commandment" (Matthew 22:36–40; Mark 12:28–33). The table of the Lord represents not just the meal that we are called to observe in remembrance of Jesus but the covenant that Jesus institutes at the table, a covenant we are called to live into in community as believers. We cannot escape this call, and when we do not follow it, we turn others away.

In recent years, most clergy have become familiar with data from the Pew Research Center. The numbers of those in the United States who choose to affiliate with religious institutions has been declining in recent decades. In the most recent report issued in January 2024, the so-called "nones"—those who have no religious affiliation—are now nearly 30 percent of respondents. What is just as alarming is that "47% of 'nones' say their *dislike of religious organizations* is an extremely or very important reason they are nonreligious. And 30% cite bad experiences with religious people. Altogether, 55% of 'nones' mention *religious organizations or religious people (or both) as key reasons for being nonreligious*" (emphasis added).[32]

The chart on the facing page makes plain that churches and church people have a real problem in making real the message of Jesus Christ. What they are saying is that religious organizations and religious people do not inspire confidence in religion or in the reality of God.

Powerful ministries and congregations have emerged that seek to serve those who have suffered "church hurt." Church hurt is not hurt that God has inflicted. Rather, it is hurt and offense that church people—people who say they are Christians and follow Jesus—have inflicted. We must be firmly committed to the practice of God's *agape* love in welcoming all to the table of the Lord. Divisions based on differences in biblical interpretation must be seen through the lens of God's limitless love. As I have tried to outline, the importance of our own spiritual growth and practice cannot be overestimated. The

---

[32] "Religion 'Nones' in America: Who They Are and What They Believe." Pew Research Center, 2024, https://www.pewresearch.org/religion/2024/01/24/whyare-nones-nonreligious/

dissonance between who we say we are and how we actually live out our ministry as church is too often glaring.

Two-thirds of 'nones' cite questioning of religious teachings, lack of belief in God as important reasons why they are not religious

*% of religious "nones" who say each of the following is an **extremely or very important reason** for why they are nonreligious:*

	Question a lot of these religious teachings	Don't believe in God	NET At least one of these
	%	%	%
All religious 'nones'	60	32	67
Atheist	83	78	91
Agnostic	78	33	84
Nothing in particular	48	19	55
Among religious 'nones' who are...			
Men	63	38	72
Women	56	25	62
Ages 18-29	65	31	69
30-49	60	35	68
50-64	58	32	67
65+	52	25	59
White	64	37	71
Black	48	19	55
Hispanic	56	20	64
Asian	51	36	59
College graduate	70	42	78
Some college	66	31	72
High school or less	46	23	52

Note: White, Black, and Asian adults include those who report being only one race and are not Hispanic. Hispanics are of any race. Estimates for Asian adults are representative of English speakers only.
Source: Survey of U.S. adults conducted July 31-August 6, 2003.
"Religious 'Nones' in America: Who They Are and What They Believe"

PEW RESEARCH CENTER

A Model for Our Movement

The questions persist: How do we share the message of Jesus Christ? Why does Jesus matter? How do we reach those who are searching for relationship with God, those who want to make a difference in the world? How can we show them that the gospel is truly about that very goal—to change the world, to show how the world can be different because of Jesus?

When we celebrate Advent, marking the season of anticipation at the coming of the Christ child whom Christians receive as God's promised Messiah, the Hebrew Bible (Old Testament) prophets share what the Messiah will be like, but they also share what the world will be like because the Messiah has come. The celebrations of Advent, Christmas, and Easter focus on the story of how God sent Jesus to earth as a child and Jesus' birth, life, death, crucifixion, and resurrection.

Resurrection is at the heart of why we believe in Jesus. Paul wrote to the church in Corinth: *"And if Christ has not been raised, then our proclamation is in vain and your faith is in vain"* (1 Corinthians 15:14). Even so, this is not the end of the story. "Christ has come, Christ is risen, Christ will come again" is a familiar phrase we say at Easter. Until Christ comes again, we must live empowered by his love, sacrifice, and resurrection and by the power of the Holy Spirit, whom he sent as a gift and helper to us. What can the world be like now that Jesus has come? Are we not called to make real that society, that kin[g]dom of God that is possible because of God's transforming power in Jesus Christ? Have we not experienced that power, that change in our own lives? Do we not want to share that transforming presence with others who are in need of love, hope, grace, and peace?

Isaiah 11 is best known as a description of the "peaceable" or peaceful kingdom. It has been visualized in many a graphic in which we see the lion lying with the lamb and all manner of animals resting peacefully together. Let's explore how this text might be a model for the movement now that Christ has come.

> *A shoot shall come out from the stump of Jesse, and a branch shall grow out of his roots. The spirit of the Lord shall rest on*

*him, the spirit of wisdom and understanding, the spirit of counsel
and might, the spirit of knowledge and the fear of the Lord. His
delight shall be in the fear of the Lord.* (Isaiah 11:1–3a)

We read here that the spirit of the Lord will rest on the Messiah,
along with the spirit of wisdom and understanding, the spirit of the
knowledge and fear of the Lord. If we are to be like Jesus, we must
also seek that spirit of knowledge and fear of the Lord. We have been
given the gift of the Holy Spirit. When we are Spirit-led, we seek and
desire to know more of God and to follow Jesus more closely. We
want to know God better. The world that is possible because of Jesus
requires that we avail ourselves of this gift of the Holy Spirit and allow
it to teach us as Jesus intended (John 14:26).

*He shall not judge by what his eyes see or decide by what his ears
hear, but with righteousness he shall judge for the poor and decide
with equity for the oppressed of the earth; he shall strike the earth
with the rod of his mouth, and with the breath of his lips he
shall kill the wicked. Righteousness shall be the belt around his
waist and faithfulness the belt around his loins.* (Isaiah 11:3b–5)

How often are we guilty of paying attention only to superficial
understandings or what others are saying or telling us about a situation?
So much of the injustice in the world is based on marginalizations: the
color of one's skin, by language, gender identity, and sexual orientation.
The dominant, unspoken narratives to which we subconsciously adhere
cause us to be guilty of misinterpreting the commands to love and do
justice. We allow humanly derived categorizations of another's worth
to somehow slide into our reading of biblical texts.

Even when we argue for a seeming statement in the biblical text that
would seem to allow for oppression and exclusion, if we are seeking
to model the Messiah, we can only read every text of the Bible with
the lens of love. There is no basis for rejecting another human being's
dignity. Whether you understand or "like" the fact that people are gay,
lesbian, transgender, or gender-neutral, you are called to treat them as
Jesus would. You may find it difficult to engage with people you find
to be racist, bigoted, misogynistic, or just plain rude. You may not be

able to abide the presence of liars or those who are dishonest in their dealings with others. And from a human perspective, you may feel you have a basis for excluding from your orbit or from the church all of the above. However, the call to love and respect others has no limits.

Even though we may express our disagreement with such persons or even our anger, we must be mindful that there is no text in the Bible that supersedes the command to love. As some of the many disciples who followed Jesus in addition to the twelve once said to themselves after hearing Jesus' teaching: "This is a hard saying—who can hear it?" (John 6:60). The world that is possible because Jesus has come requires us to do hard things. It requires us to be grounded in Spirit, Word, and prayer in order to be the people we say we are.

The most heinous criminal among us is yet worthy of human dignity, even if society has determined that punishment is warranted. Our understanding even of mass incarceration is clouded because we first have marginalized certain groups and identities, reflected in the the disproportionate numbers of Black and Brown people who are incarcerated in the United States. Black and Brown people do not commit the majority of crimes in this country; they are simply overrepresented in those who are prosecuted and punished for crime. The overwhelming majority of people who are on death row because of unjust prosecutions and unfair trials are people of color.

We have also continued to codify the vestiges of chattel slavery with our approach to how people are treated when they are incarcerated. When the Thirteenth Amendment to the U.S. Constitution made allowance that slavery was banned, "except as punishment for crime," a major loophole was created. This particular exception has given permission for incarcerated persons to be treated as chattel who are kept and caged, with little value recognized in their humanity or human potential.

The most dangerous person is yet entitled to food, shelter, and dignity, even when incarcerated. When we hear of vermin-invested prisons and jails, physical or sexual abuse by prison staff, we cannot ignore the impact of subhuman treatment on people's sense of their humanity or respect for that of others. The society in which we live now that Jesus has come *must not be guilty* of these same devaluations of human beings. Our movement to bear witness to God's love and bring justice is hypocritical if we hold to these sinful dismissals of human worth.

> *The wolf shall live with the lamb; the leopard shall lie down with the kid; the calf and the lion will feed together, and a little child shall lead them. The cow and the bear shall graze; their young shall lie down together; and the lion shall eat straw like the ox. The nursing child shall play over the hole of the asp, and the weaned child shall put its hand on the adder's den.* (Isaiah 11:6–8)

In this passage, all the animals named are natural enemies of one another. For them to eat together, let alone lie down in a vulnerable position side by side, violates what we know as the law of predator and prey in nature's food chain. Not only shall the cow and bear graze together, but their children will lie down together. Natural enemies teach their children to avoid those considered dangerous to their own existence. In a world in which Jesus has come, we have a responsibility to remove these divisions, eliminate the fear of difference, and stop putting one another in danger simply to benefit ourselves.

What has always struck me as interesting in this passage is that the "lion shall eat straw like an ox" (v. 7). Lions, I am told, do not normally eat straw, but they can digest it if it is mixed with other food elements. I think of the many experiences we have when we are seeking to build relationships with others who are not like us. If we don't like your food, we will too often denounce it as inferior. I was taught as a child that one of the more important elements of being a gracious guest is to not refuse the food that is placed in front of you. Most of us have had the experience of being served something we have never eaten before, are afraid to try, or simply have tasted and disliked. Those with good "home training" will find a way to politely explain that they simply are not hungry, are allergic, have eaten before they came, and so on. The point is that we do not denigrate the culture of others because we don't like it or we aren't familiar.

In the world that is possible because of Jesus, we will be able to respect one another's different ways of eating, singing, worshiping, and expression. We might even try, like the lion, to eat straw with the ox simply because we want to get to know the ox. We may want to try the straw because we want to show respect for the ox's culture and not disparage him because his food is different from ours. To live in a world in which there are so many differences and still reflect God's limitless love, we need to extend the abundant love and grace that God has so freely extended to us. None of us is any more valuable than any of us.

> *They will not hurt or destroy on all my holy mountain, for the earth will be full of the knowledge of the Lord as the waters cover the sea.* (Isaiah 11:9)

I hear clearly the prophet telling us that God is speaking: They will not hurt or destroy on all my holy mountain. That holy mountain is all the places where the Lord's presence is known, all the places that God has created. Imagine a world in which we do not seek to hurt or destroy. Some may see this as an unattainable fantasy. But the prophet tells us to imagine this world that is possible because of the Messiah.

How is it that this world is possible? Because "the earth will be full of the knowledge of the Lord." The knowledge of the Lord comes from seeking to know God, to know the teachings of Jesus, whom God sent to reveal God's limitless love. If we are ourselves walking humbly with God, as Micah declares God desires, if we can love as Jesus has loved us, if we seek to be like Jesus in seeking God out in prayer and in studying what God has said in scripture, then we are building knowledge of the Lord. Without such knowledge, we are left to our own human devices. Our hearts are hardened toward one another and toward justice if they have not been softened by the fellowship of the Holy Spirit and the words of scripture. It is in receiving the limitless love of God that we are compelled to share and reflect that love in the world. We may not be perfect, and we will certainly often fail. But our hearts must be under God's control, following Jesus as we seek to be his witnesses throughout the world.

In the spring of 2020, in the midst of the start of the pandemic when there were yet no known vaccines for COVID-19, we learned (several days after the fact) that George Floyd, a Black man, had been killed by a police officer who kept Mr. Floyd restrained on the ground, with the officer's knee pressed into his neck for over eight minutes. George Floyd kept saying, "I can't breathe." This was yet another unexplained murder of a Black man by police in an American city. The video that captured this murder gave us a visual we could not ignore. The inhumanity and callous spirit of the police officer came across clearly on the video. Equally disturbing was the fact that none of the police officers on the scene at the time made a move to stop the offending officer. They stood by and watched this Black man die.

All across the United States, cities erupted in anger, and some cities experienced looting and rioting, including the destruction of local businesses, as a response to yet another murder by police. Despite the fear of the COVID-19 virus, millions across America, me and my family included, strapped on our masks and took to the streets.

I was part of several nonviolent protests in Chicago. The minister of our church's Reconciliation Ministry (which leads our anti-racism efforts) and I issued a joint statement calling the nation to account and reminding our church of its commitments to fight against the injustice of racism. We held several online webinars in a series entitled "Love Is an Action Word." We invited members of the communities in our church that have often experienced injustice, racism, and marginalization to share their stories and join the call to the church to be who we say we are. Black, Hispanic, Asian/Pacific Islanders, LGBTQ+, and women; each group led one night of sharing, scripture, discussion, and prayer.

In my pain and anger, I wrote a piece that was posted on my social media account. "I want a church…" each section began. I poured out my hopes for what the church could mean in society, calling for all the ways in which the church should love. Having articulated our call to share and reflect the limitless love of God; encouraged deepening our knowledge of scripture and spiritual practice, believing that God is able to do far beyond all that we can ask or think; and committed to ensuring that we build the world that is possible because Jesus has come, I leave you with these words:

> I want a church that loves so radically that we are always putting up chairs to make room for more, always leaving empty chairs at the table, expecting that many more will come, turning no one away.
>
> I want a church that loves so courageously that we will stand up and insist that the killing of children, Black and Brown people in the U.S., and our siblings around the world must stop, and will work to enact laws and policy accordingly.
>
> I want a church that loves so generously that our priority will be the elimination of poverty, to ensure that everyone has enough to eat, safe and decent housing, healthcare, a living wage, and quality education that is not based on your zip code.
>
> I want a church that loves so creatively that we are willing to dismantle structures, traditions, and processes that dishonor humanity and marginalize any among us.
>
> I want a church that loves so completely that we are not satisfied until justice rolls down like water and righteousness like a mighty stream.
>
> I want a church that follows Jesus, and is therefore committed to work for all of this. Let's get to work, church!

May 26, 2020
Rev. Terri Hord Owens

Now to him who by the power at work within us is able to accomplish abundantly far more than all we can ask or imagine, to him be glory in the church and in Christ Jesus to all generations, forever and ever. Amen. (Ephesians 3:20–21)

REFLECTION

1. The institutional church is declining in numbers partly because political and ideological polarization has entered the church, but the Bible clearly instructs Christians to hold civil authorities accountable for the just treatment of marginalized people, such as the poor, unhoused, and discriminated against. How can a church engage in social justice and public policy advocacy without falling into the partisan polarization that the author critiques?

2. How could a church move beyond simply discussing social justice issues into taking concrete action to help "the least of these" in their local community? What specific social programs or community efforts could be supported?

3. What steps can a church take to address "church hurt" and create a welcoming environment that is authentically representative of God's love? How can a small group help to foster this kind of environment?

4. I want a church that loves radically, courageously, generously, creatively, and completely. Of these five descriptions, which one resonates most with you, and why? What are the biggest challenges a church might face in trying to embody this specific type of love in today's world?

5. Reflect on a time when you had to step outside of your comfort zone to build a relationship with someone who was very different from you. What did you learn from that experience?

6. How has this study affected your own personal understanding of what you believe about God's love? What will you carry with you as you seek to "stay at the table?"

7. What kind of church do you want? What does it look like? What does it feel like? What kind of ministry do it do? How does it embody God's limitless love?
Fill in the blanks:

I want a church that loves _____.

I want a church that _____.

www.ingramcontent.com/pod-product-compliance
Lightning Source LLC
LaVergne TN
LVHW021038300925
822264LV00007B/24